D0225408

Modern Critical Interpretations

Modern Critical Interpretations

Joseph Heller's
Catch-22

Edited and with an introduction by
Harold Bloom
Sterling Professor of the Humanities
Yale University

CHELSEA HOUSE PUBLISHERS
Philadelphia

HOUSTON PUBLIC LIBRARY

R01211 05543

© 2001 by Chelsea House Publishers, a subsidiary of
Haights Cross Communications.

Introduction © 2001 by Harold Bloom.

All rights reserved. No part of this publication may be
reproduced or transmitted in any form or by any means
without the written permission of the publisher.

Printed and bound in the United States of America

10 9 8 7 6 5 4 3 2 1

∞ The paper used in this publication meets the minimum
requirements of the American National Standard for
Permanence of Paper for Printed Library Materials,
Z39.48-1984

Library of Congress Cataloging-in-Publication Data

Joseph Heller's Catch-22/ Harold Bloom, editor.
    p. cm. — (Modern critical interpretations)
    Includes bibliographical references and index.
    ISBN 0-7910-5927-8 (alk. paper)
    1. Heller, Joseph. Catch-22. 2. World War, 1939–1945—
Literature and the war. 3. War stories, American—History and
criticism. I. Bloom, Harold. II. Series.
PS3558.E476 C334   2001
813'.54—dc21   00-050826

Chelsea House Publishers
1974 Sproul Road, Suite 400
Broomall, PA 19008-0914

The Chelsea House World Wide Web address is
http://www.chelseahouse.com

Contributing Editor: Pamela Loos

Produced by: Robert Gerson Publisher's Services, Santa Barbara, CA

Contents

Editor's Note

My Introduction finds *Catch-22* to be a Period Piece, a work for the 1960s and 1970s but not for all time.

Frederick R. Karl examines Captain Yossarian's morality, after which Minna Doskow explains how Yossarian gains a new perspective following his trip through the streets of Rome, a symbolic journey to the underworld. In separate essays, James L. McDonald and Thomas Allen Nelson probe the structure of *Catch-22*.

Stephen L. Sniderman finds that Yossarian, rather than being powerless, in fact wields more power than any other character in the novel, after which Clinton S. Burhans Jr. examines the structure of *Catch-22*, finding fault with Heller's chronology of events as related in the novel, and David H. Richter finds the theme of the novel to be that "beneath the absurdity and insanity of war lies the grim reality of death and dehumanization."

After Gary W. Davis shows how Heller uses disassociation and language to create the novel's sense of absurdity, Leon F. Seltzer argues that *Catch-22*'s absurdity is a "moral absurdity," created by a perversion of reason that prevents characters from recognizing the moral components of their behavior. Marcus K. Billson III reads the parallel between the novel and the biblical Book of Genesis, finding in the story of Man's creation the first "catch-22."

Walter James Miller describes Heller's thoughts at writing *Catch-22*, as well as two later works of fiction, *Something Happened* (1974) and *Good as Gold* (1979). In the volume's final essay, Sanford Pinsker notes that although Yossarian learns neither from his antithesis Milo Minderbinder nor from his friend Orr, he continues *trying*—and trying is what matters in *Catch-22*.

Introduction

Catch-22 (1961) after forty years is definitive of what is meant by a Period Piece, a work not for all time, but for the 1960s and 1970s. If *Catch-22* prophesied anything, it was the spirit of the Counter-Culture that began in the late 1960s and was dominant in the 1970s. By now, the Counter-Culture has been assimilated and co-opted; its principal organ is *The New York Times*. In the aura of an official Counter-Culture, *Catch-22* can be read with nostalgia (though not by me) or with the qualified patience that a four hundred fifty page extended joke demands if it is to be read at all.

Heller's half-dozen subsequent books were scarcely readable; his time had passed. World War II ended in 1945: to parody it before 1960–61 would have been in poor taste. Whether it could be parodied then, or now, is a problematic question, to which the likely answer is "No." Heller's perspective is that of individual survival, which is jeopardized by a war being run as a racket. Any perspective upon killing and being killed is legitimate, but Yossarian is not Sir John Falstaff and Joseph Heller was not Shakespeare. Madness is mocked by *Catch-22*, but the mockery loses control and enters the space of literary irreality, where only a few masters have been able to survive. Heller was not one of them.

I remember going to a performance of Heller's play, *We Bombed in New Haven*, featuring Ron Leibman, in New Haven, though I cannot recall the year. Before the intermission, I was gone, irritated by the same qualities that caused my incredulity when reviewers proclaimed *Catch-22* "an apocalyptic masterpiece." It is neither apocalyptic nor a masterpiece, but a tendentious burlesque, founded upon a peculiarly subjective view of historical reality. Subjectivity, to be persuasive, requires lucidity, and nothing in *Catch-22* is lucid. Compare Heller to the great parodist Nathanael West, and Heller vaporizes. One need not invoke *Miss Lonelyhearts*; the cheerfully savage *A Cool Million*, read side-by-side with *Catch-22*, easily eclipses Heller. After many rereadings, I uneasily laugh and wince my way through *A Cool Million*. *Catch-22*, zanily

1

comic in its motion-picture guise, no longer induces either laughter or shock.

Rather than continue to drub *Catch-22*, which will for perhaps another decade still find an audience, I prefer to meditate briefly upon the sub-literary phenomenon of Period Pieces. The Harry Potter books manifestly are for a time only; they simply are too poorly written and too weakly characterized to survive as classics of children's literature. There are permanent works of popular literature, like the detective novels of Agatha Christie, but I doubt that *Catch-22* will achieve Christie's status. Period Pieces have several distinguishing stigmata. Either they are satires or parodies whose targets have faded away (or become unassailable) or they embody stances and attitudes that reflect the spirit of a particular moment or two.

Yossarian's war ends with his departure for Sweden, a desertion that Heller presents as a triumph, which it has to be, of the war as aptly characterized by Heller's parodistic cast of con-men, schemers, profiteers, and mad commanders. War is obscene, necessarily, but the war against Hitler, the SS, and the deathcamps was neither World War I nor the Viet Nam debacle. Heller isolates the reader from the historical reality of Hitler's evil, yet nevertheless the war against the Nazis was also Yossarian's war.

FREDERICK R. KARL

Joseph Heller's Catch-22: *Only Fools Walk in Darkness*

What we yearn for in the post-war generation is fiction that seems "true"—or suggests whatever passes for truth—in its specifics as well as its generalities. While we all agree that the older great writers still move us profoundly, their vision in its particulars cannot appeal to us: Dostoyevsky was a reactionary, religious fanatic; Conrad, an anti-liberal; Lawrence, for blood, not social action; Mann, a disillusioned nationalist; Hesse, a mystic who recommended asceticism. We are still obviously affected by their psychological vision of man and the world, but repelled by what they offer in return, disturbed by the fact that they do not seem one of us. Perhaps because we have so assimilated their vision, we no longer turn to them for advice. They offer only a diagnosis, not a course of action true in its details. We read them with admiration, respect, even involvement. What they say is intensely true. But when we turn away from their printed pages, we face a different world. They are too idealistic for us. They want too much change, and at best they offer only spiritual rewards.

On the other hand, a novel like *Catch-22*, trailing recollections of Joyce, Nathanael West, and early, "funny" Céline, speaks solidly to those who are disaffected, discontented, and disaffiliated, and yet who want to react to life positively. With its occasional affirmations couched in terms of pain and cynical laughter, it makes nihilism seem natural, ordinary, even

From *Contemporary American Novelists.* © 1964 by Southern Illinois University Press.

appealing. The very zaniness of its vision constitutes its attraction even to those who have compromised with most of the absurdities it exposes.

Catch-22 obviously appeals to the student, who beneath his complacency and hipster frigidity is very confused and afraid. It appeals to the sophisticated professional—the educator, lawyer, professor—who must work at something he cannot fully trust. It appeals to the businessman, who does not really believe that his empire primarily serves the public good. It certainly appeals to all the new professionals—the advertisers, publicity men, television writers—whose world is little different from the absurd one Heller presents.

Wartime life on Pianosa—whatever the veracity of its details—is a replica of life within any organization. Whether one is a lawyer, teacher, doctor, judge, union member, white collar worker, or writer attached to a magazine, advertising agency, newspaper, or television station, he finds himself in a similar kind of world. It is not simply a neurotic reaction to his surroundings that gives one this sense of absurdity: the absurdity is an actual fact, the consequence of many conflicting interests interacting and creating a world unfit for the individual.

This point is of course true of all good service fiction, but is particularly true of *Catch-22*, beginning with its catchy title, its sense that the individual must always relinquish part of himself to the organization which chews him up and them eliminates him. Most people try to prevent becoming waste matter. The novel appeals to all those who want the good life and nevertheless reject its particularities, or even fear defining them. Beneath the surface, all its avid readers are afraid that "life"—whatever it is—is dribbling away from them in ways they can never dam. Calling themselves social animals, and arguing that every individual must be part of society, they hate society and distrust any individual who is a social animal.

For those who find given life nauseating, frustrating, and demeaning— that is, our sane citizens—*Catch-22* provides, at least temporarily, a moral, affirmative way out. So far do people diverge from their public image that their frustrated longings often consume their entire existence. They may wish to do right, but are compromised by the wrongness of their situation. They see themselves as defeated victims, but are forced to carry themselves as victors. They want to love, but find that hate is more sophisticated, and viable. They want to pursue self, but are admonished and shamed into embracing the public good. They desire to aid society, but are warned that only a fool puts self last. They wish for authenticity, good faith, decency, but find that inauthenticity brings immediate and often sensational results. Trying to believe, they more frequently are mocked by the very forces they desire to accept. Wishing to embrace the great world, they find themselves successes in the little.

What American novel of the last decade has spoken better to this type of individual—perhaps to all of us?—than *Catch-22*? Its surface extravagance masks a serious purpose: that in an impossible situation, one finally has to honor his own self; that in an absurd universe, the individual has the right to seek survival; that one's own substance is infinitely more precious than any cause, however right; that one must not be asked to give his life unless *everybody* is willing to give *his*.

It is the latter point—a kind of Kantian categorical imperative applied to survival—that has generally been neglected. When Yossarian decides that his life does count, he is making a moral decision about the sanctity of human existence. Life must not be taken lightly, either by others (military men, business manipulators, world leaders) or by oneself. Yossarian is a hero by virtue of his sacred appraisal of his future. To himself he is as valuable as a general or a president. Since he is so valuable, he has a right, an inviolable right, to save himself once he has done his share of the world's dirty business. The individual must consider himself supreme. What could be more democratic, American, even Christian!

Heller's point is always moral. The fact that many outraged readers saw Yossarian as immoral, cowardly, or anti-American simply indicates what falsely patriotic hearts beat sturdily beneath seemingly sophisticated exteriors. Yossarian is a great American—if we must have this point—an American of whom we should all be proud, even if Heller makes him an Assyrian (at times he seems like a Young Turk hiding behind an Armenian name).

The morality, in fact, both implied and stated, is somewhat pat. Despite the presence of so many seemingly "evil" characters, Heller believes implicitly in the goodness of man. Even the former (Cathcart, Dreedle, Milo, *et al.*), however, are not really evil in any sinister way: rather, they simply react to the given chance, the proffered opportunity. They could be professors, or even ministers. They are men on the make, and such is the quality of modern life *all* men are waiting for their chance. There are millions of Eichmanns, Hannah Arendt tells us. Yossarian is a Jesus among the money-lenders, without the mean sense of righteousness of a potential Messiah.

Yossarian is the man who acts in good faith, to use Sartre's often-repeated phrase. In Yossarian's situation—one in which war has turned all men into madmen—people float uneasily in a foreign world where human existence is feeble, contradictory, and contingent upon an infinity of other forces. Nothing, here, is certain except the individual's recurring assurance of his own response. All he can hope to know is that he is superior to any universal force (man-made or otherwise), and all he can hope to recognize is that the universal or collective force can never comprehend the individual.

The only sure thing in a swamp of absurdity is one's own identity. "I think, therefore I am" has never seemed truer, distorted though Descartes' phrase may have become in the twentieth century.

Accordingly, the true hero of our era is the man who can accept absolute responsibility. He must act alone, and his faith—not in God, but in himself—must be good, honest, pure. If, as Nietzsche said, all the gods are dead, then man must become mature enough to assume the role. Yossarian's decision that life must pre-empt all other considerations is precisely this moral act of responsibility. In choosing life, Yossarian shows himself to be reflective, conscious, indeed free. All the others are slugs living in the swampy depths of self-deception; not bad men necessarily, they are simply unaware, and unaware they cannot be free.

When Yossarian strikes for freedom at the end of the novel (the fact that it is Sweden demonstrates Heller's concern with the good society made by good men), his act symbolizes more than defiance, certainly not cowardice. He has done his duty—Heller is careful to keep before us Yossarian's many missions (the word itself indicates a high calling). He has shown his responsibility to society at large, and has given his physical energy and his nervous sweat. Now he must seek a meaningful life, try to make order out of chaos. He must overcome nausea. In this respect, Sweden seems like Paradise: sane people, plenty of good sex, a benevolent government, jolly drunkenness. In Sweden, the individual seems to have a chance, what Yeats felt in part about his mythical Byzantium.

It is no more immoral for Yossarian to seek Sweden than for Yeats to have searched for Byzantium. Both places indeed are more a state of mind than a real place. We can be sure that when Yossarian reaches Sweden, he will be disappointed, even frustrated. Not all the tall, blonde women will capitulate, not all the people will be sane; the government will even expect him to work, and liquor will be expensive. Yet Sweden remains valid as an idea—one certainly has the right to seek it as an alternative to death. It may prove a false Eden, but man in his desperation may still desire Paradise. It is a mark of his humanity that he does.

There is, except for Sweden, really no community that Yossarian can join. An open character in a closed society, he must shun everyone to retain his identity: appear naked among the clothed, refuse to acquiesce to ill-motivated orders, avoid love while seeking sex, reject a mission that is no longer his. In virtually every situation, he is alone—his name, his racial origin, his integrity all indicate his isolation. Like an ancient hero rather than a modern *schlemiel*, he goes through his solitary ordeal, and the ordeal, as Heller presents it, is eminently worthwhile: to defy death in the name of reason and life.

A good deal of the humor of the novel derives from Yossarian's very openness in a society closed to authenticity and good faith. When an open character—responsive, sensitive, decent—throws himself upon a closed society—unresponsive, fixed, inflexible—very often the result can be tragic. What keeps Yossarian comic, however, is the fact that he never tries to change the society he scorns; he is quite willing to accept its absurdity if it will leave him alone. Never a revolutionary, rarely a rebel, unintentionally a hero, only occasionally a young Turk, Yossarian is more often a rank conformist. The only sanity he desires is his own, not the world's; the only joys he seeks are those he can himself generate; the only rewards he covets are the compensations, not of glory, but of full lips, breasts, and thighs. He is more Sancho than Don. The comedy of Yossarian is the comedy of a romantic, Rousseauistic natural man forced to do the dirty work of the world.

Yet this twentieth-century natural man is "with it," not against it. He is able to adapt to the forces that would otherwise destroy. He retains his naturalness (integrity, sexual balance, coolness) in situations that have frustrated and smashed men more rebellious and affirmative than he. What both impresses and dismays us is Yossarian's adaptability; his views do not cause rigidity, and without rigidity there can be only personal comedy. Tragedy is always "out there," involving those who try to fight the system or those who are trapped by a system they never understood (Clevinger, Nately, Snowden). Like Yossarian, Milo is of course comic because he *knows* about the system; he is the very fellow who masterminds systems.

The two extremes Yossarian must avoid include the avarice and egoism of Milo and the innocence and naïveté of Nately ("new-born") and Snowden (pure whiteness). As Heller presents the alternatives, a person must be in the know in all the particulars of life or else he cannot be true to himself. Only a fool walks in darkness. Yossarian is an honest man because Yossarian understands that the way to righteousness is through balance: he must assure his own survival without the help of others. Thus, Heller condemns both Nately and Milo; the latter obviously stands for a base, commercial acquisitiveness, while the former attempts to be Jesus Christ in a situation that calls for an instinctive sense of survival.

Those who have felt the tragic overtones of the novel often find it difficult to place its tragic center. Clearly, *Catch-22* is not simply a comic novel full of puns, highjinks, slapstick, witty dialogue, and satirical asides. It has these in abundance—perhaps, on occasion, in overabundance—but its purpose and execution are fully serious, what we feel in Saul Bellow's work, to mention a contemporary American whom Heller comes closest to. At the center of the tragedy is Heller's awareness of a passing era, an era that perhaps never existed but one that might have if people and situations had gone differently. Heller's is the nostalgia of the idealist—such a writer's style is usually jazzed-up, satirical, somehow surrealistic—the idealist who can never accept that moral values have become insignificant or meaningless in human conduct. This heritage, what we find in Nathanael West, early Céline, and a whole host of similar writers, derives from the tragic undertones of Ecclesiastes with its monody against vanity, egoism, hypocrisy, folly—those qualities which have, unfortunately, become the shibboleths of the twentieth century.

Heller's recoil from these false qualities takes the form of his attack upon religion, the military, political forces, commercial values—as C. Wright Mills indicates, the whole power formation of a country successful in war and peace. What is left is the only true thing remaining for all men—sex: healthy, robust, joyful sex. Not love—Heller carefully draws the distinction—for love means entanglements and involvements that will eventually lead to phoniness. It is not so curious that love itself falls victim to a society in which true feeling had better stop at orgasm. Heller's non-treatment of love is of course indicative of his attitude, not of an inability: love is martyred amidst people whose every feeling is promiscuous. To expect more from them, even from Yossarian, is to accept their folly as truth.

The nightmarish scenes of *Catch-22* which convey its tragic sense culminate in the cosmic nightmare of Chapter XXXIX, "The Eternal City." Once glorious, Rome is now a "dilapidated shell," as though modern Goths and Vandals had destroyed everything in their path; or as if a modern God had visited his wrath upon it. The monuments are shattered, the streets contain surrealistic nightmares, the people seem the husks and shards of humanity. All values are overturned, all hopes and dreams made valueless; sanity itself becomes a meaningless term. Everything visible—an emblem of what lies beneath—is off balance, out of key. The center of western religion is godless. Here we have Heller's immoral world, a scene from Hieronymus Bosch's Hell, in which Aarfy can freely rape and kill while Yossarian is picked up for lacking a pass. Caught in such a dark world, Yossarian can only run toward the light. If he stays, he will—like Milo and the others—eat and sleep well at the expense even of those who share his ideals.

An early version of *Catch-22* was itself much more nightmarish in its development than the published book. Evidently strongly influenced by *Ulysses*, Heller had originally tried to make the narrative typically Joycean: that is, full of intermittent streams of consciousness and involutions of time. Further, he suggested the narrative through recurring symbols of devastation and doom, eliminating in several places orthodox plot structure. As a consequence, the reader who missed the significance of the symbols—and they were by no means clear, even peripherally—was lost in a surrealistic forest of words from which there was no escape. Added to the stream, the symbols, and the involutions of time was an impressionistic treatment of characters and events, a half-toned, half-tinted development that seemed neither to go forward nor to remain still.

For the final version, Heller retained in its entirety only the first chapter of the original and then in part straightened out both the narrative line and the character development. Words themselves became a kind of language midway between evocation and denotation; at its worst, the language overextends itself, but at its best it suits Heller's zany, absurd world. So often misunderstood, his language would not of course fit a rational theme—it is itself an attempt to convey a world beyond the logic of the word.

For Heller, the war is a perfect objective correlative, as it was for Hemingway in *A Farewell to Arms*. Both, however, are war novels only in limited ways. The war gave Heller, even more than it did Hemingway, the community against which Yossarian can operate. The military becomes an entire society, looming so large that it casts its shadow on the horizon and blocks out everything beyond. Such is the nature of the curse, and it is this—the indefinable character of what one is a part of—that Heller can exploit. The war or the military (not the enemy) provides the conflict, makes anything possible. The norm is no longer any determinable quality: each action gives birth to a norm of its own. Unlike the fixed roles that people assume in civilian life, in war they hide behind masks (uniforms) and redefine themselves, like the protean creatures in Ovid's *Metamorphoses*. Here, Yossarian—the ancient Assyrian, the modern Armenian, but really a wandering New York Jew—can give vent to his disgust and revulsion, and through laughter show us that our better selves may still turn up in Sweden.

MINNA DOSKOW

The Night Journey in Catch-22

Sanford Pinsker in his article on *Catch-22* characterizes Heller's hero as a *puer eternis*. As a result, he sees Yossarian refusing the "traditional journey of learning in manhood," and the ending of the novel becomes Yossarian's escape from reality to Sweden, a kind of never-never land. Although Yossarian may be innocent, as Mr. Pinsker claims, at the beginning of the novel, and his belief that he can work within the establishment using their rules for his own ends is incredibly naïve, he does, I believe, learn better, and after his symbolic journey to the underworld, represented by his trip through the dark streets of Rome, he comes to a new recognition of the meaning of his experience and reaches a new knowledge in the hospital after his near death, achieving what one could perhaps call an informed innocence. His flight to Sweden is not an escape but an alternative as he himself tells us: "I'm not running *away* from my responsibilities. I'm running *to* them." Thus, a definite and meaningful pattern of action emerges from the novel, and one which is startlingly similar to the archetypal pattern that characterizes classical epic or romance. Heller's hero, like those of *The Odyssey*, *The Aeneid* and *The Divine Comedy*, is involved in a struggle with an alien force which he must and eventually does overcome in order to survive. He too reaches a crisis in his struggle, undertakes a journey to the underworld, emerges with new knowledge, and is finally victorious, prevailing against the forces

From *Twentieth Century Literature* 12, no. 4. © 1967 by IHC Press of Immaculate Heart College.

marshalled against him. From the outset of the novel, Yossarian struggles against a hostile establishment and the code it maintains for controlling the society it rules, that is, Catch-22, the principle of power which states "they have a right to do anything we can't stop them from doing." However, the confrontation reaches its climax and emerges most clearly and intensely in the night journey episode of the last chapters, and in the action that follows from it. A close analysis of these chapters (39–42) will show how Yossarian through his participation in the archetypal pattern of the descent and renewal of the romance hero achieves his new perception which culminates quite logically in his flight to Sweden.

When Yossarian goes AWOL to Rome in an attempt to save the kid sister of Nately's whore, we witness a crisis in his continuous battle with the establishment. In his previous conflicts with those forces, Yossarian was consistently foiled by 'Catch-22.' However, his absolute and unconditional refusal to fly any more missions after Nately's death indicates a new and complete break with the code 'Catch-22' typifies. In the subsequent trip to Rome his efforts are not only directed at saving his own life, but also those of future generations represented by the still virginal twelve year old sister. "Every victim," he tells us in explaining his action, "was a culprit, every culprit a victim, and somebody had to stand up sometime to try to break the lousy chain of inherited habit that was imperiling them all." He is out to break the "mind-forged manacles" that imprison men. While this enemy is far different from the medieval dragon or classical monster whom the romantic hero must overcome, yet it is equally menacing to human life, can prove equally fatal, and Yossarian must overcome it in order to achieve his own renewal.

As he plunges into Rome, a city of universal destruction, Yossarian begins his symbolic descent to the underworld. At first he tries to enlist the aid of the authorities in control. But his initial naive attempt to work with the Roman police is blasted by their essential indifference and by Milo Minderbinder's preference for black-market tobacco profits to the salvation of little girls. Yossarian, realizing that the police will not help him, then begins the journey on his own. However, since it is a journey born out of pure frustration it is cast in a somber and ironic rather than a truly romantic mode. He has already learned that he can expect no help from the police, and before his journey is over he will further discover that the police themselves are the enemy and that he must protect himself from them.

His emergence from the police station leaves him at the bottom of a hill in a "dark tomblike street," obviously suggestive of an entrance into the underworld with its murky atmosphere smelling of death. However, it is not an otherworldly or spiritual hell but the hell that man has created both spiritually and physically here on earth that Yossarian enters. And what the reader sees as he accompanies Yossarian on his harrowing night journey through the labyrinthine streets of this Roman hell is:

> all the shivering stupefying misery in a world that never yet had provided enough heat and food and justice for all but an ingenious and unscrupulous handful.

Nevertheless, the striking atmosphere of misery and pain leads to the inevitable comparison with hell which becomes more relevant and forceful as Yossarian travels further along the streets encountering sickness, hunger, poverty, sadistic cruelty and coercion and viewing an entire gallery of mutilated bodies and warped souls.

The pervasive gloom through which Yossarian travels resembles Dante's City of Dis or Homer's City of Perpetual Mist in its absence of penetrating light. In scene after scene of his journey, from the yellow light bulbs that "sizzled in the dampness like wet torches" immediately outside the police station, to the "ghostly blackness" and "dense impenetrable shadows of a narrow winding side street," through the "drizzling, drifting, lightless, nearly opaque gloom," the darkness remains impenetrable. Even the apparent sources of light cannot shatter the gloom. The yellow light bulbs do not enable Yossarian to look around him, and the "flashing red spotlight" attached to the M.P.'s jeep only adds a lurid glow to the picture of the young lieutenant in convulsions. Nor do the amber fog lights of the ambulance which is used to incarcerate the helpless victims of the police light up the scene, and even the street lights themselves appear as "curling lampposts with eerie shimmering glare surrounded by smoky brown mist." The only exception, the piercing white light of Tony's restaurant, is expressly forbidden to the ordinary inhabitants of Rome and to Yossarian as well and is clearly marked "KEEP OUT."

Not only is Yossarian cast into a world without light, but the city itself appears strangely distorted and out of perspective. "The tops of the sheer buildings slanted in weird surrealistic perspective and the street seemed tilted." The lampposts seem to curl, and together with the mists the shadows succeed in "throwing everything visible off-balance." The shimmering uncertainty of forms helps to upset Yossarian's equilibrium and enhance the unearthly quality of the scene through surrealistic distortion.

Even the elements conspire to intensify the hostile and bizarre nature of the setting. From the outset Yossarian finds himself pelted by a frigid rain, exposed and vulnerable, denied shelter and forced to huddle for warmth and protection against the raw night. Moreover, the rain does not, as might be expected in another region, cleanse what it touches, but only besmirches it.

Thus the street is "rain-blotched," the mist is "smoky brown," and Yossarian stumbles upon "human teeth lying on the drenched glistening pavement near splotches of blood kept sticky by the pelting raindrops poking each one like sharp finger nails." The rain lends this street a bloody luminescence intensifying the gory and grotesque scene, and the drops themselves seem to sharpen the probing cruelty.

The distortion of the visible world surrounding Yossarian is accompanied by an equal distortion of all that is audible. Just as the yellow bulbs outside the police station lend the street an eerie light, so do the sizzling sounds they emit echo the effect. However, the most common sounds that Yossarian hears as he travels through the streets of Rome are human cries, the sobs and screams of the victims of hell. The scream of the child being beaten, the sympathetic weeping of a woman in the crowd, the "snarling, inhuman voices" of the spectators, the cries of the women being raped begging "Please don't," or in drunken variation "Pleeshe don't," the scream of the man being clubbed by the police, "Police! Help! Police!" all swell the chorus of pain, the cacophony of hell. In addition, the accents of the torturers are also audible and add to the clamour. We hear the hellish accents of the M.P.'s who mock and jeer at the suffering young lieutenant in "raucous laughter."

Even inanimate objects take on the disturbing characteristics of their surroundings. Announcing its arrival with jangling clamour, the ambulance is distorted into an engine of torture, not a vehicle of mercy, and it comes not to aid the soldier with the mutilated mouth, but to incarcerate the screaming civilian who clasps his books to him in an uneven struggle with the club-wielding policemen arresting him. The fountain which Yossarian hopes will help guide him out of hell is dry, and becomes a perfect symbol of the aridity and barren aspect of the surrounding wasteland. The "haunting incongruous noise" that Yossarian hears of a snow shovel scraping against a rain soaked street adds a weirdly surrealistic note suggesting the meaningless and endless labor of some modern Sisyphus.

The labor of hell is characteristically unproductive, endless and pointless. Thus, the labor represented by the sound of the scraping shovel is adapted to its location as is the aimless action of the six soldiers trying to help the epileptic young lieutenant. In their well-intentioned impotence they only succeed in moving him from car hood to sidewalk and back again achieving nothing. The realization of the futility of their attempts to alleviate his pain and help their friend and of the inevitable isolation of the suffering man cause "A quiver of moronic panic [to] spread from one straining brute face to another." Their effort is unproductive and his isolation remains unaffected.

The only actions that yield results in hell are cruelty and coercion. While the soldiers are powerless to relieve the suffering of their sick friend, the M.P.'s can mock it and so intensify it. And, in the same way, the sympathetic woman is powerless to stop the man from beating his dog and must retreat "sheepishly with an abject and humiliated air" from the sadist's stick which can easily be turned against her. The crowd watching the child being beaten has already recognized the limits of action, and thus no one moves in even a futile attempt to stop the beating. No one here still hopes to avert the surrounding cruelty, and the sympathetic only weep "silently into a dirty dish towel."

As Yossarian proceeds further and further into hell on his journey, he witnesses a progression in the inhumanity and brutality that surrounds him. The figures he sees become more horribly maimed, the mutilation becomes more inclusive and extensive, and the possibility for action more limited. The imagery proceeds in a crescendo of distortion and pain until it excludes all possibility of redemption or love, and even the futile attempts to help that he observed toward the beginning of his journey are absent. Yossarian, much like Dante in his progress through the Inferno, thus passes through the various levels of hell necessary for his final emergence as a new person having learned his proper course of action on the verge of entering a new realm. Moreover, accompanying the progression in Yossarian's surroundings, is a progression in Yossarian's own role in the action, again necessary if he is to learn from his hell journey.

Although Yossarian is, from the beginning, haunted by his surroundings and feels compassion for the souls he sees in torment, he is not an integral part of the hell he walks through. He is an alien observer proceeding in "lonely torture, feeling estranged," isolated although not insulated from his surroundings. He feels a sense of his own difference and of alienation from those around him.

> . . . he thought he knew how Christ must have felt as he walked
> through the world, like a psychiatrist through a ward full of nuts,
> like a victim through a prison full of thieves.

The perception fills him with dread and he tries to escape from the world surrounding him. However, despite his efforts to flee, there is no escape until he has gone through all of hell and until his isolation too has been broken down. In spite of all his efforts not to see and not to hear what is around him, he cannot avoid the sights and sounds of torment, and each turning only takes him farther into the labyrinthine hell of the Roman streets. Even when he sights a familiar landmark, the dry fountain, which he believes will guide him to the officer's quarters, he manages only to come upon another instance of brutality: the man beating the dog. Unlike Raskolnikov, whose dream this scene reminds him of, Yossarian cannot dispel the terror by awakening. The nightmare world is his reality and he must go on in this world observing repeated torments until he recognizes this and recognizes his own involvement in that world as well.

Only after Yossarian comprehends the warning shout uttered by one of the victims of the police:

> "Police! Help! Police!" . . . a heroic warning from the grave by a doomed friend to everyone who was *not* a policeman with a club and a gun and a mob of other policemen with clubs and guns to back him up.

when he recognizes the forces that control the world for what they are, does a distinct change occur in his role. For the first time in his journey, Yossarian ceases to be the alien observer isolated from his surroundings. He feels the threat extended to himself as well as to the others around him, identifying him somewhat with them. He also recognizes a direct possibility for action, a distinct opportunity to help the old woman of eighty with the bandaged ankles who is chasing the burly woman half her age. But he responds in the same way as the other inhabitants of hell. Like the passive crowd watching the beating of the child, he does nothing. His failure to act identifies him more closely with the shade-like victims he has observed, and now he no longer observes the action from outside but from within it. This change in his role makes him flee not in dread this time, but in shame since he recognizes his identity with those around him and shares their guilt. Thus, "he darted furtive, guilty glances back as he fled in defeat." He, like all the other inhabitants of Rome, has given in to the forces in control and is defeated since he has allowed the principles ruling hell to rule him as well. Brought to acknowledge that "mobs with clubs were in control everywhere," he also now admits that he has neither the power nor the will to oppose them. This explicit recognition of his defeat foreshadows his later capitulation to the Colonels (the ruling minions of that enormous and organized "mob with clubs"—the army) who embody the extension of the ruling principle in the hellish world beyond Rome.

Yossarian, no longer separated from the world around him, is tortured in the same way as the figures he has passed. The only image that he can salvage from the picture of universal corruption is the memory of Michaela, the plain, simple-minded and hard working maid who served in the officers' apartment and who had somehow retained her innocence amid her savage surroundings. His rush towards her is a last attempt to save himself from complete despair. However, only her violated and mutilated body lying on the pavement is there to welcome him, "the pitiful, ominous, gory spectacle of the broken corpse." Aarfy has already raped and murdered her. Thus, the one apparent departure from the picture of universal deformity and perversion has become the sacrificial victim of that deformity and perversion. The demonic distortion that has corrupted the world culminates in the image of Michaela's maimed body, the rape and killing of the one girl associated with the army who was not a whore, and the final resolving chord in the demonic crescendo that has been building throughout the journey is sounded.

In a further change of role which reiterates his position at the inception of the journey, Yossarian, no longer the observer, no longer passive, challenges the world around him in a last appeal for justice and order, for the vindication of humane ideals. He shouts: "you can't take the life of another human being and get away with it, even if she is just a poor servant girl." It is inevitable that this appeal be denied by the forces in control. Thus, morality is finally and completely turned inside out; moral law or justice has completely degenerated into rule through naked power; the "mobs with clubs" are in full control, and "mere anarchy is loosed upon the world." As the agents of retribution are heard on the stairs and Aarfy slowly turns green in anticipation of punishment, Yossarian's absurd hope that order will be restored to the chaos he has been wandering in all night is blasted. The "two large brawny M.P.'s with icy eyes and firm sinewy unsmiling jaw" who appear act in perfect consistency with hellish logic and with 'Catch-22.'

> They arrested Yossarian for being in Rome without a pass.
> They apologized to Aarfy for intruding and led Yossarian
> away between them, gripping him under each arm with fingers as
> hard as steel manacles.

As if to emphasize the metamorphosis of humane law into its demonic opposite, the M.P.'s no longer retain even their superficial humanity; their flesh having turned to steel, they resemble unyielding machinery rather than men.

After Yossarian has personally experienced the rule of the demonic principles as well as observed their universal application, he consents to become a part of this rule. Thus, as his actions in relation to the old woman of eighty have intimated, he accepts Colonel Korn's and Colonel Cathcart's "odious deal," knowing it is disgusting and deceitful. At this moment he is rechristened with a hellish name, taking on a new and appropriate identity.

"Everyone calls me Yo-Yo!" he tells us, accepting a name he once found noxious.

When he accepts the Colonels' deal after his return from Rome, Yossarian is for the first time in the novel in complete harmony with his environment. He has joined in the devilish conspiracy that holds sway over the world and whose undisguised sinister image has been evident throughout the novel, although most clearly and intensely seen in the night journey episode. Having then sunk into hell itself, no longer resisting its influence but becoming part of it, a lost soul himself, Yossarian approaches the absolute depths of the abyss and glimpses a demonic phantom. This is the "strange man with the mean face," the "spiteful scowl," the sharp fingers, the "nasty smirk" and "malicious laugh" who eludes Yossarian's grasp and will only say, "We've got your pal, buddy. We've got your pal." Nor will he elucidate when Yossarian, with a flicker of sardonic humor on Heller's part, inquires "What the *hell* are you talking about?" (Italics are Heller's.) However, we must remember that Yossarian is still anesthetized at the moment of his vision. Thus, his physical state of induced unconsciousness partially accounts for his new submissive attitude. It also corresponds to his spiritual or moral state in which consciousness has as well been put to sleep temporarily, as exemplified in his acceptance of the "odious deal." In this state he can see the devil without really recognizing him or perceiving the meaning of his message. The vision is nevertheless vital to any new perception Yossarian will be able to achieve after the both literal and figurative anesthesia wears off.

After his vision, Yossarian once more rebels and refuses the Colonels' deal. He emerges, in this way, from unconsciousness and from the abyss into whose depths he had to descend before his renewal or resurrection could occur. Just as Dante descends into the nethermost region of hell, passes Satan himself, and uses the devil to pull himself out of hell, so Yossarian uses his Satanic vision to extricate himself from his hell in order finally to approach a place where there still is hope. In both cases the contact with the devil is mandatory. As Virgil tells Dante, "There is no way/but by such stairs to rise above such evil."

After he passes the devil whose words recall Snowden's death to him, Yossarian glimpses the truth which gleams from the haunting memory: "The spirit gone, man is garbage." He now realizes that it is necessary to retain some other quality along with the mere existence that he has been struggling to preserve since the beginning of the book and that he had guaranteed through his "deal." Armed by his recent experience in hell and his emergence from it through the recognition of what life means, he has once more achieved the strength to say no to the tyrants in control. "I'm not making any deals with Colonel Korn," he tells us. Unlike his earlier instinctive rebellion, his new denial is informed by the experience of the depths of hell and by his new recognition. Only through his exploration of the abyss has he reached the perception which may lead to his eventual salvation. And it is possible salvation that is offered by Yossarian's projected plan of flight to Sweden. Perhaps it is only Purgatory that Yossarian will gain (as Dante does at this point in his progress), but it is a world where life is at least possible.

Yossarian now realizes that accepting the Colonels' deal would be, in his words, "a way to lose myself," would be, that is, his own damnation through complete surrender to the demonic powers in control. But what he is searching for is a way to "save" himself (to use his own words again) in a world that both he and Major Danby, the university professor turned army officer, agree contains "no Hope." This last phrase is reiterated throughout their entire discussion of escape so that we can hardly fail to think of the cardinal feature of hell and also of the motto that Dante tells us is inscribed over the gates of hell. In addition, Heller's language heightens our awareness of the scene's implications. The words "lose," "save," and "no hope" echo rather forcefully the conventional religious language describing the soul's struggle for salvation. From the latter we know that hell is a place of no hope and that it is a spiritual state as well as a geographical location. We know that the lost soul goes to hell and conversely, that hell is the condition of the lost soul. And finally, we know that the soul can only achieve salvation by recognizing evil and resisting or overcoming it. It is obvious how appropriately this describes Yossarian's progress in the novel, shown most clearly in the chapters just discussed.

Thus, Yossarian's departure for Sweden is the concrete external representation of his spiritual renewal that expressed itself first in his recognition of man's nature and in his subsequent refusal of the "deal." As Yossarian knows, Sweden is no paradise or utopia; there are no such things in the world this novel depicts. In escaping to Sweden, Yossarian also recognizes that he is "not running away from responsibilities," but toward them, that salvation entails responsibility, and that he will have to be ever-vigilant in order to remain free of the demonic powers of the world he is forsaking. Thus he leaves taking the necessary risks and exulting in the new feeling of freedom and hope that he now has. If it is a miracle as the chaplain claims, then it is a miracle achieved through Yossarian's own will and conscience and one which leaves him open to ambush and knife attack from such characters as Nately's whore. It is she who marks his departure from the demonic realm, his crossing of the gulf, she who is herself caught in the endlessly repeated and repeatedly unsuccessful actions characteristic of hell, and who thus represents the threats that Yossarian will have to overcome on his new course.

JAMES L. McDONALD

I See Everything Twice!:
The Structure of Joseph Heller's Catch-22

"I see everything twice!" today's college student scrawls on the last page of his bluebook to signify that he had a bad day. "You've got flies in your eyes," he mutters at the campus policeman or the dormitory prefect. "Where are the Snowdens of yesteryear?" he asks, referring to a friend who has flunked out, been drafted, or suddenly made the Dean's List after two years on probation.

The use of the quotations testifies to the impact *Catch-22* has made since its publication in paperback just over four years ago. Like *The Catcher in the Rye*, *Lord of the Flies*, and *A Separate Peace*, Joseph Heller's novel has become one of those books which college students take up as their own, from which they draw the slogans which are meaningful to them in relation to the established power structures they live under.

I suspect, however, that students admire *Catch-22* for the wrong reasons. Though the book is in tune with the restlessness and rebelliousness of the times, and though the "Catch Cult" rightly praises its black humor and its anarchic (even pacifist) tendencies, it is not merely a book which reflects and forms current college opinion. It is a novel, and it seems time to discuss it as a novel: to examine, in some detail, its formal values.

On a first reading, *Catch-22*—switching its focus from one character to another, whirling crazily through a hodgepodge of slapstick antics, bizarre

From *The University Review* 34, no. 3. © 1968 by the Curators of the University of Missouri-Kansas City.

horrors, grotesque anecdotes, and aimless digressions—may well make the reader try to rub the flies out of his eyes and wonder where the Snowdens of yesteryear or any year fit in. But close analysis reveals that Heller is a highly sophisticated, conscious artist who carefully manipulates the diverse and seemingly divisive elements of the novel to achieve structural unity: that discernible pattern which gives the reader a firm sense of the time, place, and thematic relevance of each unit in the novel, so that he knows where he is at each point in relation to where he has been before.

Ironically, the reader's bewildered "I see everything twice!" provides the key to the relation of the parts to the whole, what Chaplain Tappman calls "*Déjà vu*": "For a few precarious seconds, the chaplain tingled with a weird, occult sensation of having experienced the identical situation before in some prior time or existence. He endeavored to trap and nourish the impression in order to predict, and perhaps even control, what incident would occur next, but the afflatus melted away unproductively, as he had known beforehand it would. *Déjà vu.* The subtle, recurring confusion between illusion and reality that was characteristic of paramnesia fascinated the chaplain, and he knew a number of things about it."

This is a remarkably clear description of the method Heller employs. Obviously, he is not dealing with this "characteristic of paramnesia" scientifically; but he is using the phenomenon as the basis of the novel's structure. Out of the welter of digressions, flashbacks, and anecdotes, he constructs his narrative and contrives thematic patterns so that the reader has the experience of seeing everything twice—the sensation which the chaplain calls "*Déjà vu.*"

"*Déjà vu*" is, first of all, an explanation of and a reason for Heller's narrative construction. An artificial chronology of the novel's action can be worked out: the action proper begins with Yossarian's training in Colorado; it proceeds through his combat missions over targets like Avignon and Bologna, and the death and disappearances of his comrades; it is marked by Milo Minderbinder's rise to power and the raising of the missions from forty to eighty; and it culminates in Yossarian's refusal to fly any more missions, his discovery of the real meaning of "Catch-22," and his desertion.

The actual narrative, however, is not chronological. Heller—like Proust, Joyce, Virginia Woolf, and Faulkner—is the heir of Henri Bergson: he does not view time as something dependent on and made relevant by the artificial orderings of the clock or the calendar; rather he regards it as something governed and made tangible by the consciousness of the individual, his situation, and his memory. The past operates in the present by forming the individual's apprehension of the present, coloring and outlining each significant moment.

Thus Heller begins the novel in the middle of things, just beyond the midpoint of Yossarian's career as a bombardier when, in the hospital after flying forty-four of the required fifty missions, he meets the chaplain. From this point on, the action alternates between what happened before the opening of the novel, and what happens after it. Heller interweaves past and present, the past action continually crowding into the present. A character or situation in the present is outlined; then, through free association with some aspect of the character or situation, an event from the past, in the form of an anecdote, a digression, or a flashback, sweeps into and obliterates the present. This event, in turn, frequently merges with or flashes off to still another event. The past event, however, is seldom related as one complete, coherent unit. Rather the reader learns of it partially, in disjointed fragments: he has the "sensation of having experienced the identical situation before," the desire to "trap and nourish the impression," and the frustration of seeing "the afflatus" melt "away unproductively." Only tentatively and gradually can he reconstruct it, place it in relation to other events in time, and understand its significance.

The story of Snowden's death exemplifies Heller's technique. In Chapter Four, the reader learns the bare facts, that "Snowden had been killed over Avignon when Dobbs went crazy in mid-air and seized the controls away from Huple"; but then the account shifts to the intrigues of Colonels Cathcart and Korn. In the following chapter the incident is recalled, and the reader learns that Dobbs had broken radio silence with a plea to help Snowden, who lay dying in the back of the plane; but then the incident is dropped. It is not taken up again until Chapter Twenty-One, where some of its significance is hinted at: during the story of how Yossarian stood naked to receive the Distinguished Flying Cross, Captain Wren explains that "'A man was killed in his plane over Avignon last week and bled all over him . . . He swears he's never going to wear a uniform again.'"

In the following chapter the reader discovers that "Yossarian lost his nerve on the mission to Avignon because Snowden lost his guts," hears Snowden's plaintive "I'm cold," and sees him "freezing to death in a yellow splash of sunlight near the new tail gunner lying stretched out on the floor . . . in a dead faint"; but again the account shifts, this time to the story of Dobbs' plan to murder Colonel Cathcart. In similar fashion, additional information about the death of Snowden is supplied in subsequent chapters. Not until the second-last chapter of the novel, however, is the whole story reconstructed. In the hospital, Yossarian—bathed in an "icy sweat" which reminds him of Snowden—recalls the entire event and remembers "Snowden's secret" that "Man was matter," that "the Spirit gone, man is garbage."

One can describe the novel's overall construction, then, as an interplay between present narrative and the cumulative repetition and gradual clarification of past actions. The interplay portrays, dramatically, the manner in which the characters apprehend their world, and shows the impact of the past on their present attitudes and actions. Each moment in the present flashes their minds back to fragmentary images of past events which influence their behavior so heavily. The reader's gradual and partial realization of the nature and significance of past events matches those "weird . . . sensations" which the chaplain characterizes as *Déjà vu*.

Déjà vu further provides the basis for the method Heller uses to contrive the thematic patterns of the novel. He manipulates the characters, events, and situations into elaborate parallels which, through comparison and contrast, clarify and illustrate the novel's central themes. He thereby gives the reader the sensation of seeing everything at least twice, of "having experienced the identical situation before" because it parallels other situations or is related to others thematically.

Heller carefully sets two worlds in opposition to each other: the world of those in power, and the world of their victims. Revolving the action around that "subtle, recurring confusion between illusion and reality" which the chaplain notes, he centers the themes of the novel on the question of human identity. By a series of parallels, he clarifies the concerns and attitudes of both groups. Those in power attempt to succeed within an artificial system by adhering to its ethics, which reduce human beings to abstractions, statistics. Their victims attempt to preserve their identities by rebelling against the system—either through parody, or outright defiance.

The official attitude of those in power is outlined very clearly by the doctor who persuades Yossarian to pose for the parents of the dead Giuseppe as their son:

> "They [the parents] didn't come to see me," Yossarian objected. "They came to see their son."
> "They'll have to take what they can get. As far as we're concerned, one dying boy is just as good as any other, or just as bad. To a scientist, all dying boys are equal."

For "scientist" the reader might well substitute "bureaucrat" or "officer" (or "Scheisskopf," the name signifying the role of all officers), or simply "those in charge." This is the official attitude: those in charge view all human beings as "dying boys," statistics, means to an end. Employing the crews as their pawns, they wage a constant battle for position and glory.

Heller illustrates the attitude by paralleling the motives and methods of the officials along the entire scale of army rank.

The novel is marked by a series of bids for power, which the reader sees again and again. At the highest level of rank is the struggle between Generals Dreedle and Peckem. Just below it is the rivalry between Colonels Cathcart and Korn, with Cathcart's ambitions epitomizing the irrationality and pedantry of those who attempt to rise in the system. Cathcart treats all crews—"dying boys"—alike: he raises their missions and volunteers the squadron for the most dangerous assignments, not to help win the war, but to attain glory and promotion. His letter of sympathy, in the jargon which marks all the official communiqués in the novel, typifies his attitude:

> *Dear Mrs., Mr., Miss or Mr. and Mrs. Daneeka: Words cannot express the deep personal grief I experienced when your husband, son, father or brother was killed, wounded or reported missing in action.*

On a lower level there are Captain Black's loyalty oath crusade and the plots of the C.I.D. men. Finally there are Gus and Wes, who treat all patients alike, painting their gums and toes purple and forcing laxatives down their throats, regardless of the ailment. Triumphant over them all, of course, is Milo Minderbinder, whose Enterprises virtually make him ruler of the world, who regards whole armies as means to his end, impartially contracting to bomb both the Allies and the Axis for the profit of the syndicate.

The victims of the officials are bewildered and virtually helpless. They live in a world which, in keeping with the attitudes and actions of the officials is irrational and inexplicable. As the warrant officer with malaria complains, "'There just doesn't seem to be any logic to this system of rewards and punishment.'"

There is no real logic within a system manipulated by those who have the right of "Catch-22" which says "'they have a right to do anything we can't stop them from doing.'" Thus Major Major Major becomes, almost automatically, Major Major Major Major and, by official whim, is made squadron commander; the dutiful Major Metcalf is shipped to the Solomon Islands to bury bodies; Dunbar is "disappeared"; the patriotic Clevenger and the innocent Chaplain are ruthlessly interrogated; Chief White Halfoat is the victim of the government and the land-grabbers; Yossarian is arrested for being in Rome without a pass while Aarfy, the murderer, goes free.

All the dying men are treated alike and all men—in war—are dying. The dying, the dead, have no real identity—only official status. Death and life are merely matters of official routine: the question is decided, not through recourse to reality, but by reference to official lists and records.

The parallel incidents involving the soldier in white, Mudd, and Doc Daneeka typify the predicament. It is impossible to tell whether the soldier in white is dying or dead: wrapped up in plaster and gauze like a mummy, he is no more than a helpless unidentifiable victim. Equally helpless are Mudd (whose name signifies his fate) and Doc Daneeka. Mudd, the dead man in Yossarian's tent, was killed in combat over Orvieto; but according to official army records he is alive because he never officially reported for duty. Doc Daneeka, in reality, is alive; but according to official lists he is dead because he was officially listed, though not really present, in the crew of the plane which McWatt flew into the mountain. Heller explicitly links the three victims, indicating the deliberate parallelism he sets up.

Yossarian complains that "'Anybody might be in'" that case of plaster and gauze that is the soldier in white: "'For all we know, it might even be Mudd!'" Leter, Sergeant Towser laments that "now he had *two* dead men on his hands—Mudd . . . who wasn't even there, and Doc Daneeka . . . who most certainly was there and gave every indication of proving a still thornier administrative problem for him."

The problem the victim faces in maintaining his identity centers most obviously on Major Major Major, whose identity is fixed by a perverse practical joke: "It was a harsh and stunning realization that was forced upon him at so tender an age, the realization that he was not, as he had always been led to believe, Caleb Major, but instead was some total stranger named Major Major Major about whom he knew absolutely nothing and about whom nobody else had ever heard before. What playmates he had withdrew from him and never returned, disposed, as they were, to distrust all strangers, especially one who had already deceived them by pretending to be someone they had known for years. Nobody would have anything to do with him."

His identity determined by the official list—the birth certificate— Major Major Major is abandoned by all. He has no real identity of his own; his fellow officers suspect that he is Henry Fonda. He becomes the perpetual outcast, one whose very existence is dubious. Finally he retires into bizarre seclusion, completely withdrawn from the squadron: he can only be contacted in his office when he is not there; when he is there, no one is permitted to enter.

Major Major Major's actions reduce the official attitude to absurdity, parodying it by turning it upon itself. Throughout the novel, the victims— and Major Major Major must be numbered among the victims, even though he is a high-ranking officer—attempt to preserve themselves by adopting masks designed to thwart the official attitude, to take advantage of the I.B.M. mentality of those in charge. Both Major Major Major and Yossarian pose as Washington Irving when they carry out official duties. Major Major Major takes the pose further by signing himself as Irving Washington, John Milton, or Milton John on official documents. Yossarian, in order to remain safe and secure in the hospital, adopts the identities of Warrant Officer Homer Lumley, Giuseppe, and A. Fortiori.

These masks belong to a pattern of acts of rebellion against the system, some comic, others deadly serious. As the novel progresses, the victims, growing more and more aware of the menace of the system, carry gestures of rebellion to the point of outright defiance. Yossarian—with the chaplain the moral conscience of the novel—is most blatant in defiance of the system: his moaning during the Avignon briefing, and his query "'Where are the Snowdens of yesteryear?'"; his insistence that there is a dead man in his tent; his nakedness after the Avignon mission and during the presentation of the medal; his efforts to halt the Bologna mission by putting soap in the squadron's food and moving the bomb line; his repeated requests to be grounded, his final refusal to fly any more missions, and his desertion. The system, as such, cannot be lived with. It cannot be changed. It cannot be thwarted, beyond a certain point. The only way to overcome "Catch-22" is to run away from things—to commit an act of treason, desertion in the face of the enemy. All of the action and the events of the novel point to this conclusion.

Throughout *Catch-22*, then, Heller is using *Déjà vu* as the basis of the methods by which he achieves structural unity. Constructing a narrative interplay between the past and the present, contriving elaborate parallel repetitions of and variations on his central themes, he enables the reader to say, with Yossarian, "'I see everything twice!'" He creates the discernible, ordered pattern which is of the very essence of art.

THOMAS ALLEN NELSON

Theme and Structure in Catch-22

Many early critics of Joseph Heller's *Catch-22* have damned it either outrightly or with faint praise, lashing out at the novel with such epithets as a "jabberwock of a work," "nightmarish," "mildly eccentric," "scrambled," "an emotional hodgepodge," and, according to Whitney Balliett's *New Yorker* review, a novel containing only "a debris of sour jokes, stage anger, dirty words, synthetic looniness, and the sort of antic behavior a child falls into when he knows he is losing our attention." Until recently, critics have tended to disparage the artistry of the novel on the grounds that it contains too many gratuitous features: repetitiousness, loose structure, unnecessary subterfuge. Such criticisms of the novel's apparent structural and thematic incoherence are answered to some extent by Minna Doskow's interesting analysis of Yossarian's final flight. Doskow argues that the structure of *Catch-22* resembles the archetypal pattern of the classic epic or romance, and that the novel's resolution represents a symbolic journey to the underworld (in Yossarian's final trip to Rome), resulting in Yossarian's recognition of responsibility. Doskow, therefore, suggests a relationship between the theme of Yossarian's escaping *to* responsibility and the structure of the novel. Instead, however, of a standard romantic structure of descent and ascent, I think, as Heller himself has suggested, that *Catch-22* has a cyclical pattern of action which complements the multifarious ideas and issues associated with the theme of responsibility.

From *Renascence* 23, no. 4. © 1971 Catholic Renascence Society, Inc.

Of crucial importance in critically estimating Heller's thematic mastery and specifically the theme of responsibility is an understanding of the world of *Catch-22*. How is it portrayed? What are its values, its concept of order, of right and wrong, of man's place in the universe? Notice, for instance, the manner in which Heller represents authority on the island of Pianosa, a setting which suggests a microcosm of the modern world and to which Heller attaches some symbolic meaning on the novel's title page: "The island of Pianosa lies in the Mediterranean Sea eight miles south of Elba. It is very small and obviously could not accommodate all of the actions described. Like the setting of this novel, the characters, too, are fictitious." Authority on this island seems ethereal, hermetic, and tyrannical. Authority embodies a "system," or Establishment, which is inimical to individual welfare, a system which Yossarian views as the ubiquitous "they." Yet, Yossarian, the empiricist and sometimes idealist, reasons that "they" do exist—"strangers he didn't know shot at him." Because this society appears as mysterious and chaotic to a sensibility such as Yossarian's, judgments of importance come not from exalted authority, but from individual experience. What appears to Yossarian as pestilential insanity, however, symbolizes an arena for action and achievement to those who incorrectly believe they exercise some control over the course of their fates. The men of power and responsibility—Peckem, Dreedle, Cathcart, and their legion—attempt to impose some sense of order on the chaos, but when ex–pfc Wintergreen and those who have access to the mimeograph machine make crucial decisions, when Scheisskopf, a fatuous ass who excells in the system, regiments order in parades, we realize that in this society ruthless cunning or accidents of IBM fortune make right, not concepts of just law, individual freedom, or moral responsibility. Order in the system achieves its epiphany in Scheisskopf's toy soldiers and in the universality of M&M Enterprises.

Heller, obviously appalled by the prospect of an Armageddon, examines what results when no rational and humane basis for life exists in a world which harbors a military arsenal capable of destroying civilization. In view of such a situation, a society in which purblind men pursue their own advancement at any cost becomes absurd, destructive, and totalitarian. Clevinger's idealism fails him because the people in whom he has too much faith betray his trust by their willingness to apply power and selfish ambition as bludgeons to justice.

Heller develops several themes which grow out of his depiction of a world of irrational and absurd contradictions. *Catch-22* contains an appearance-reality theme, one common to works which deal with the disparity between a given society's consensus values and irresponsible practices. Major Major's background taught him those humanistic values of freedom, compassion, and goodness common to Christianity and the American democratic tradition, when, in reality, his society subscribes to a competitive and callous devotion to oneupmanship. Individuals within Major Major's society demonstrate all the residue of the American Dream: they marry, have children, are successful and ambitious, and yet they are the progenitors of psychological tensions far beyond their comprehension or control. Major Major's fear of recognition and responsibility results from an insidious protestant ethic which preaches the sanctity of human life but which condones human slaughter in the name of philistine expansionism, patriotism, and prejudiced fear. Major Major's primary failing, from his society's viewpoint, is his lack of insensitivity to these moral contradictions. As a result, Major Major is universally disliked as a "flagrant nonconformist."

For every Major Major in the system stand multitudes like Colonel Cathcart. Cathcart combines a plethora of contradictions: "He was dashing and dejected, poised and chagrined . . . complacent and insecure, daring in the administrative stratagems he employed to bring himself to the attention of his superiors and craven in his concern that his schemes might all backfire." While Major Major will stop at nothing to annihilate his identity, Cathcart will do anything to create an identity which might ameliorate his stature within the system; all his aborted identities contribute only to his paranoia, infantilism, and moral vacuity. Because of an insatiable ambition to be a general—a laudatory aim in his society—Cathcart views reality through the distorting perspective of chauvinistic bombast and in consequence his action conforms to dogma and fantasy rather than to reality. He constantly turns to Colonel Korn for the assurance that consensus absolutes are inviolable ("Atheism is against the law, isn't it?") while, in reality, his fate depends upon an administrative Russian roulette and the capricious whims of his superiors.

The most crucial theme, therefore, which emerges from the depiction of such a social system concerns the inability to pin down moral responsibility in a world which summarily witnesses and perpetrates the devaluation of human life. Who—or what—is responsible? Acts are accomplished with a certain degree of efficiency: planes take off, drop bombs, destroy people and property, all of which requires some form of organization and decision-making. Major Major abdicates the responsibility of his office (one which he did not seek) yet "whatever he was supposed to get done as squadron commander apparently was getting done without any assistance from him." Is the responsible party Major —— De Coverly, a man who passes the majority of his time pitching horseshoes, kidnapping Italian laborers, and renting apartments to soldiers? De Coverly displays remarkable ingenuity by being the first on hand to get his picture taken following a city's liberation and by being the one who casually undermines Captain Black's Great Loyalty Oath Crusade. For all his recognition, however, Major De Coverly assumes no responsibility; this seeming enigma comes to represent nothing more than just another rapacious war profiteer.

In order to enlarge upon the theme of responsibility (or irresponsibility) within the system, Heller highlights the activities of Milo Minderbinder. Milo, not content with the operation of one mess hall, works for both the Germans and the Allies, revealing in the process the contradiction between patriotic rhetoric and the capitalistic search for expanding markets. Like De Coverly and other characters of position, Milo refuses to bear any responsibility for the deaths and misery which his enterprises may inadvertently cause. Mudd, the man who never was, dies over the bridge at Oriveto as a result of Milo's informing German antiaircraft of the American mission. Milo's rationale speaks for itself: "'I didn't kill him!' Milo kept replying passionately to Yossarian's angry protest. 'I wasn't even there that day, I tell you. Do you think I was down there on the ground firing an antiaircraft gun when the planes came over?'" That he did not actually pull the trigger, to Milo's thinking, exonerates him from any culpability in the death of Mudd, or later, in Snowden's death, whose pain could not be alleviated because Milo had removed the morphine from the first-aid kit, leaving only a note which testifies to an incredulous and malign innocence: "What's good for M&M Enterprises is good for the country."

If Heller depicts this world as a welter of evil, what, then, is his concept of man's relationship to the larger forces in the universe? Perhaps Yossarian's ruminations on death, hospital style, defines Heller's point:

> They didn't take it on the lam weirdly inside a cloud the way Clevinger had done. They didn't explode into blood and clotted matter. They didn't drown or get struck by lightning, mangled by machinery or crushed in landslides. They didn't get shot to death in hold-ups, strangled to death in rapes, stabbed to death in saloons, bludgeoned to death with axes by parents or children, or die summarily by some other act of God. Nobody choked to death. People bled to death like gentlemen in an operating room or expired without comment in an oxygen tent. There was none of that tricky now-you-see-me-now-you-don't business so much in vogue outside the hospital, none of that now-I-am-and-now-I-aint.

The *Weltanschauung* of *Catch-22* chronicles a medieval world of suffering, misery, and death without a forgiving God as the trump card. In the place of

God and redemption rises the system, defining life and death with a fusillade of charts, statistics, feathers in caps, and black eyes. If Nurse Cramer had read the thermometer correctly, the Man in White might have lived, if Colonel Cathcart had prayed less for tighter bomb patterns and more for human lives, great suffering might have been spared. The Warrant Officer's cynicism ("who gives a shit?") epitomizes the feelings of characters who have no faith in the possibilities of justice, whether human or divine: "Just for once I'd like to see all these things sort of straightened out, with each person getting exactly what he deserves. It might give me some confidence in this universe." This position rejects even experience, not just particular moral systems, believing that a morality based solely on experience produces an absurd determinism which contradicts itself from one day to the next.

The search for value in *Catch-22*—and such a positive element does exist in the novel—does not tread epistemological or ontological paths. What Heller initially stresses through those characters concerned with an ethical approach to experience—Yossarian, Orr, the Chaplain, characters with little position or power at stake—is their examination and rejection of consensus values which are no longer tenable (if they ever were). Those values tainted with self-aggrandizement, greed, or national gain in a world which could destroy itself, Heller—and a handful of his characters—considers infantile and self-righteous. Milo's free enterprise morality, Major Major's father's protestant ethic, Nately's patriotism and jingoism—all of these shibboleths—are no longer logical, moral, or practical. Yossarian, through individual protest, discovers an alternative to these values. When all possible corrective action is cut off and if ignoble conformity or rebellion are the only choices, then the recalcitrant individual must protest, even if flight becomes the only feasible manifestation of his dissent. Because the system defines reality through administrative machinations ("they can prepare as many official reports as they want and choose whichever ones they need"), Yossarian cannot stay and fight. Instead of merely representing a quixotic gesture, Yossarian's and Orr's flight stands as a positive renunciation of officialism and as an assertion of individual conscience.

Instead of being content with satiric nihilism, Heller promulgates a moral and ethical system which is basically humanistic and rational: man, a creature capable of reason, has a moral responsibility to oppose irrationality and inhumanity in his social and political institutions by demanding a rational code of ethics based on the needs of human beings living in a changing and potentially volatile world. The present system, he argues, with its outmoded approach to modern life, an approach which does not distinguish between means and ends, dehumanizes essential human relations. Man, when abstracted, impersonalized, and mechanized, loses the best features of his humanity: his desire to know truth, to create a rational and humane civilization, to realize and fulfill his need for love, to develop his capacity for creative endeavors. Instead, what the system offers as sexually ideal is characterized by the lurid paradise of flesh in the whorehouses of Rome, which assumes the guise of masculine fantasy. Or, in contrast to whorey pulchritude, Heller presents the indifference and frustration of the nurses. With Nurse Duckett, because no verbal or emotional rapport exists, Yossarian relishes the concrete sexual act: "He thirsted for life and reached out ravenously to grasp and hold Nurse Duckett's flesh."

This dehumanization process stands out in a medical motif which runs throughout the novel. Early in *Catch-22*, an unnamed colonel is examined, fingered, prodded, and dissected by a circle of specialists: "The colonel dwelt in a vortex of specialists who were still specializing in trying to determine what was troubling him. They hurled lights in his eyes to see if he could see, rammed needles into nerves to hear if he could feel. There was a urologist for his urine, a lymphologist for his lymph, an endocrinologist for his endocrines, a psychologist for his psyche, a dermatologist for his derma. . . ." Man, in a scientifically oriented society, can become only matter, a squalid object, like Mudd and the Man in White, without spirit or identity. Human beings, as illustrated by Aarfy's murdering of a servant, cease to be morally responsible agents and become garbage to be tossed out windows. And, to a scientist, "all dying boys are equal." This motif complements Heller's repetitious use of imagery which suggests death by obliteration and which culminates in Snowden's "secret": "It was easy to read the message in his entrails. Man was matter, that was Snowden's secret. Drop him out a window and he'll fall. Set fire to him and he'll burn. Bury him and he'll rot like other kinds of garbage. The spirit gone, man is garbage. That was Snowden's secret. Ripeness was all."

To complement this complex interplay of ideas of motifs associated with the theme of responsibility, Heller constructs *Catch-22* through a series of what he calls, in an interview for *The Realist*, "recurring cycles." Events and characters which may be outrageously funny when first introduced acquire philosophical significance in the last part of the novel as the degeneration of values increases to alarming proportions. This structural device leads not to unnecessary repetition, as many have argued, but to an expansion of moral awareness in Yossarian and reader.

Chapters 1, 17, and 34 form such a cycle. One of several significant details in this cycle is the Man in White, who, when initially introduced, contributes to a prevailing sense of incredible absurdity: "A silent zinc pipe rose from the cement on his groin and was coupled to a slim rubber hose that carried waste from his kidneys and dripped it efficiently into a clear, stoppered jar on the floor. When the jar on the floor was full, the jar feeding his elbow was empty, and the two were simply switched quickly so that stuff could drip back into him." Yet, when Heller, in Chapter 17, returns to the same point in time, the Man in White, like human experience, takes on new dimensions as enlarged perspectives are applied. Now Heller characterizes him as a "stuffed and sterilized dummy," a figure symbolic of the lack of existence in the system. The events between these two chapters (2–16) lend credence to this interpretation by cataloguing such details as Cathcart's paranoia, Doc Daneeka's greed, the reduction of men to machines ("sightless, stupid, crippled things"), Hungry Joe's sexual frustration, Havermeyer's sadism, Kraft's parades, Black's Crusade, Aarfy's insensitivity, and a blatant devaluation of human life within the system. In Chapter 34, Dunbar cries "he's back" and properly allegorizes the Man in White's function in the novel: "He's hollow inside, like a chocolate soldier. They just took him away and left those bandages there." The Man in White symbolizes the ubiquitous, unknown, indeterminate non-entity who is so much a part of the system—and our society—and who, without his powers of sensibility and reason, represents simply another organism which takes matter, absorbs it, and excretes it or uses it up.

Significant in these recurring scenes is the setting of the hospital. In all three of these chapters, the hospital serves as a safe asylum from the outside world for Yossarian and Dunbar. Whereas in Chapter 1 we might view Yossarian as a profane and irresponsible malingerer, by Chapters 17 and 18 his "liver ailment" increases in thematic importance. When Yossarian realizes that the Soldier Who Saw Everything Twice is faking, he reverts to illusion for the purpose of survival; the hospital furnishes Yossarian the illusion of safety where, at least, death is more predictible and less messy than on the outside. Throughout most of the novel, Yossarian searches not so much for truth or moral responsibility, but for a bower of bliss. By Chapter 34, the hospital no longer represents a place of sanity (Dunbar is "disappeared") and, in Yossarian's last hospital stay (Chapter 41), Colonel Korn hovers over him while a team of doctors debate whether to cut him to pieces or not. Yossarian realizes that these illusions are not satisfactory—the system can still get to him in the hospital and in the whorehouses of Rome. Yossarian's final flight, unlike his earlier ones, symbolizes not one of illusory escape, but one of protest. Sweden represents an objective to move toward— and one fraught with danger—in order to change an intolerable situation.

In the final eight chapters of *Catch-22* (35–42), Heller completes and ties together a multitude of cyclical patterns which he so carefully establishes in the earlier parts of the novel. In Chapter 35, the development of Milo's role in the novel reaches its climax. At the nadir point of his development, Milo's ambitions seem harmless and even laudatory. In Chapter 7, Milo wants to serve the best food possible, a seemingly admirable adjunct to his belief in the free enterprise system. Yet, as Milo's political power extends as a result of his economic coups (Chapter 22, "Milo the Mayor"), Heller indicates how apparently harmless ambitions can shape values and attitudes which make men insensitive to human suffering. At Snowden's funeral (Chapter 24), Milo's concern for finding a market for his Egyptian cotton creates an impenetrable barrier between himself and Yossarian's despair. Snowden's death, like the travails of humanity in general, means nothing to Milo, while, to Yossarian, it represents a revelation of some kind. While Yossarian yearns for some understanding of human misery, Milo searches for loopholes and legal outs. Whereas Yossarian attempts to interpret life ("it's the tree of life"), Milo remains the literalist ("no, it's a chestnut tree"). And, finally, there emerges Milo the Militant (Chapter 35) who thrives, as does private enterprise, on war and its rhetoric. The novel's last reference to Milo (Chapter 42) implies that others—like Cathcart and Wintergreen—who could not lick him decided to join him. By this time, Yossarian has nothing to turn to for help but the inspiration of Orr's escape.

Chapter 36 ("The Cellar") brings two thematically crucial cycles into better perspective. When, in Chapter 1, Yossarian ends one of his censored letters with "I yearn for you tragically, A. T. Tappman, Chaplain, U.S. Army," he implicates the Chaplain in his Washington Irving deception. Similarly, throughout the novel, Yossarian and the Chaplain are linked together by their mutual quest for some light on the nature of reality (the Chaplain, characteristically, sees his search in terms of a religious quest) and through their sensitivity to human suffering. Like Yossarian, the Chaplain has his illusions—the "naked man" in the tree (Yossarian) as mystical revelation, the mysterious Flume as prophet of the woods (Chapter 25). These "mystical experiences" stimulate a renewed hope in the Chaplain but they are only valuable as indications of his inevitable rejection of private mysticism for rational humanism. The Chaplain's tie with Yossarian enlarges as the novel progresses and returns to particular motifs: the Washington Irving game, the naked man in the tree, and even his faking Wisconsin shingles (Chapter 34) bind the Chaplain's fate with that of Yossarian's. "The Cellar" allegorizes the theme that men are bound together irrevocably through their actions and that in apparently innocent and childish acts of rebellion, such as Yossarian's signing letters Washington Irving and A. T. Tappman, the moral responsibilities which one man has toward another can be breached. Ironically, the Chaplain, perhaps the most selfless man in the novel, feels guilt for crimes against the system which exist only in his disturbed imagination and in Cathcart's paranoia. The genuine miracle for the Chaplain occurs in Chapter 42 when he knows that Yossarian and Orr have escaped: he gains some courage and a sense of purpose in the knowledge that the system can be beaten—that "Catch-22" is fallible.

As Yossarian and the Chaplain gain knowledge, the system evolves into more phrenetic forms, so that by Chapter 37 Scheisskopf (now a general) symbolizes the absurdity and increasing degeneracy of a world without rational law, without justice, without its humanity. Through an administrative error (paper realities have replaced all other realities), Scheisskopf takes charge. Everyone—except those fortunate enough to escape—will march!

The sense of allegory which pervades the later chapters increases in Chapter 38, the chapter in which Nately's Whore attempts to kill Yossarian and in which Yossarian concerns himself with the fate of Kid Sister. Earlier in the novel, the whorehouse scenes furnished some excellent satire on the meaninglessness of war (the Old Man's debate with Nately in Chapter 23) and generally satirized masculine, sexual fantasies (Aarfy, for instance, bragging of never having "paid for it"). Nately's puerile attempts to metamorphosize his whore into homogenized American nubility demonstrates how cultural myth overpowers reality. In Chapter 38, however, the "whores" can no longer be dealt with purely on the basis of our own masculine stereotypes—they develop into human beings who, like Snowden, are matter, who suffer pain, and who deserve better treatment. Yossarian assumes responsibility for Kid Sister because no one else does. Perhaps the fantastic sequences in which Nately's Whore attempts to kill Yossarian can be explained symbolically by the fact that she, being unschooled in the sophistry of the system, knows that someone must be responsible for Nately's death and Yossarian happens to be available. Thus, Yossarian, like Christ, assumes responsibility for those sins which others in the system refuse to acknowledge.

Not until Chapter 39 ("The Eternal City") does Heller attach a symbolic meaning to Rome other than as just another place for Yossarian to find respite from his fear of death. Like the hospital, Rome is not immune to the death, disease, and destruction which increases in the novel in direct proportion to Yossarian's enlarged awareness. Yossarian, as a compassionate knight-errant, views the ruins of Rome, from the whorehouse to the Colosseum, with a philosophical disgust not known to him earlier in the novel. Heller uses this setting as an allegory of an earlier civilization which, like ours, tolerated and perpetuated the exploitation and destruction of human life, except that now death is acted out on a grander scale and with a larger cast, so that Aarfy's unconcern for the death of one girl reduces all human life to insignificance: "I hardly think they're going to make too much fuss over one poor Italian servant girl when so many thousands of lives are being lost every day."

If anything, then, *Catch-22* is constructed meticulously, even, as Heller says in an interview for *The Realist*, "with a meticulous concern to give the appearance of a formless novel." The final three chapters (Chapters 40–42) complete the treatments of Snowden's death and his "secret" and Yossarian's final resolution to flee toward responsibility. At this point, a definite technique can be discussed and outlined: in the beginning of the novel, Heller treats people and incidents as though they were glimpses (Snowden's death, for example), and then he demonstrates that these actions and characters seen as glimpses at the first do have meaning and that they do come together; he stresses the point that people's acts are interrelated in an inescapable sort of way, that we are all bound by the same moral laws, and that all of us are linked to one another by the acts which we perform (or fail to perform); the novel's settings and situations do not necessarily represent America, but seemingly a monolithic world which closes off every conventional avenue of protest or corrective action and which, because it perpetuates many of the obsolete values of past generations, could easily reduce human civilization to a wasteland. Yet, to Yossarian, the answers seem so simple and so evident, but communication breaks down and a frightening sense of frustration prevails. Such frustration comes to the surface in a succession of scenes where characters are indifferent (they don't even care when they are poisoned by the soap in the potatoes), where people both physically and mentally cannot do anything, where, in short, human beings feel helpless in the face of total moral irresponsibility and insanity. With their will to resist gone, their moral courage sapped by fear, characters only have faith in the infallibility of "Catch-22," the god of the insane, an unwritten, unseen law which gives efficacy and decree to all the indifference and injustice in the novel. Like Yossarian, we know "Catch-22" does not exist— that human inequities require responsible human solutions—but does everyone else?

STEPHEN L. SNIDERMAN

"It Was All Yossarian's Fault": Power and Responsibility in Catch-22

There are so many villains and power-mongers in *Catch-22* that it is easy to minimize or overlook Yossarian's culpability in the world Heller describes. The characters in the novel who are most often cited as the "real" controllers of Power are Milo Minderbinder and ex-P.F.C. Wintergreen. Jan Solomon believes that Milo "begins the novel as a hard-working young hopeful dreaming of a syndicate and ends wielding absolute power." Joseph J. Waldmeir feels it is ex-P.F.C. Wintergreen "who, for all practical purposes, runs the war from his clerk's desk by manipulating orders and memoranda." To Sanford Pinsker both of these characters "ultimately evolve as the real manipulators of power in *Catch-22*." Yossarian, on the other hand, is generally identified with the powerless. James L. McDonald, discussing a group that obviously includes the protagonist, claims that "the victims of the officials are bewildered and virtually helpless." Gerald B. Nelson says that Yossarian "sees what is wrong, the corruption that greed and envy have brought in their wake, but he can do nothing save run away."

In one sense, of course, these positions are unchallengeable. Milo and Wintergreen, or their real-life counterparts, must have greatly influenced the outcome of the war, while the Yossarians undoubtedly had little effect at all. In the fictional sense, however, it is Yossarian who controls things, not Wintergreen or Milo. In one way or another, Yossarian is responsible for

---

From *Twentieth Century Literature* 19, no. 4. © 1973 IHC Press of Immaculate Heart College.

nearly every significant event mentioned in the novel, including most of the deaths we witness. Within the framework of the novel, Yossarian cannot be considered the helpless victim of a monolithic system. In fact, he wields more potential power than any other character in the book. Until he learns to use it, however, his efforts to save himself from destruction are not only futile, but lead to catastrophe and death for those around him. The irony of the novel is that Yossarian is unaware of his power and spends much of his time blaming others—Cathcart, Milo, "they"—for his predicament. What Yossarian learns in the course of the book is that he, and no-one else, is in control of his fate. The novel seems to be designed to hide this fact from the reader until Yossarian himself sees it. The world in which he exists is made to appear inescapable and uncontrollable, but the sequence of events we are shown and Yossarian's relationship to them indicates that he is the center of his universe and, though he does not know it at first, capable of turning it topsy-turvy or setting it straight.

In Chapter nineteen Colonel Cathcart makes a list of "Black Eyes!!!" Next to two of the items, "Ferrara" and "Naked man in formation (after Avignon)," he writes "Yossarian!" Next to the other items, "he wrote in a bold, decisive hand:

?

Those entries labeled '?' were the ones he wanted to investigate immediately to determine if Yossarian had played any part in them." Of course, Yossarian did play a part in making every item on the list (with the exception of "Skeet Range") a "Black Eye" for Cathcart. He moved the bomb line on the map during the Great Big Siege of Bologna, had Corporal Snark put laundry soap in the sweet potatoes which caused the "Food Poisoning (during Bologna)," started the "Moaning (epidemic of during Avignon briefing)," and encouraged the chaplain to hang around the officers' club every night.

But Yossarian's influence is even more pervasive than Cathcart's list indicates. He is directly responsible for Dobb's decision not to murder Cathcart and for Nately's broken nose. His habit of signing Washington Irving's name to the letters he censors eventuates in the appearance of two C.I.D. men on the base and the subsequent interrogations of Major Major. His signing of the chaplain's name to one letter lends to the brow-beating of the chaplain in the cellar of Group Headquarters. The punch that Yossarian receives from Appleby (after Orr had smashed open Appleby's forehead with his ping-pong paddle) causes Chief White Halfoat to bust Colonel Moodus in the nose, which in turn causes General Dreedle to have the chaplain thrown out of the officers' club and to order Chief White Halfoat moved into Doc Daneeka's tent. Yossarian also provides the impetus for Milo's international cartel, as James M. Mellard points out, since it is Yossarian's letter from Doc Daneeka authorizing him to get all the fruit he wants which makes it possible for Milo to start his syndicate.

More significantly, Yossarian can be linked to the deaths of many of his acquaintances. He is most clearly responsible for the deaths of Kraft, his crew, and Lieutenant Coombs, who were killed over Ferrara: "the bridge was not demolished until the tenth mission on the seventh day, when Yossarian killed Kraft and his crew by taking his flight of six planes in over the target a second time." Earlier we had been told about "Lieutenant Coombs, who had gone out on a mission as a guest one day just to see what combat was like and had died over Ferrara in the plane with Kraft." Since Yossarian is responsible for Lieutenant Coombs's death, he is "responsible" for Chief White Halfoat's presence on Pianosa and therefore for the living death of the "ghostly" Captain Flume who was driven to live by himself in the forest by Chief White Halfoat's threat to slit his throat from ear to ear.

Yossarian's responsibility for Mudd's death can also be established. Mudd was killed over Orvieto when "Milo contracted with the American military authorities to bomb the German-held highway bridge . . . and with the German military authorities to defend the highway bridge . . . with antiaircraft fire against his own attack." Obviously, Milo is to blame for Mudd's death—although he denies it vehemently by saying, "I wasn't even there that day"—but Yossarian could have prevented the fiasco by stopping Milo from buying the entire harvest of Egyptian cotton when they were in Cairo together and eliminating the need for a money-making scheme like the Orvieto contract. Wintergreen asks Yossarian why he let Milo buy all the cotton in the world: "'Me?' Yossarian answered with a shrug. 'I have no influence on him.'" But Yossarian's rationalization is as weak as Milo's. It is Yossarian, after all, who convinces Milo to give up the idea of chocolate-covered cotton and to bribe the government instead. And it is to Yossarian Milo comes when he needs advice or comfort: "Milo was even more upset by the possibility that someone had poisoned his squadron again, and he came bristling fretfully to Yossarian for assistance." On the trip to the Middle East, in fact, Milo tells Yossarian: "'That's what I like about you,' he exclaimed. 'You're honest! You're the only one I know that I can really trust.'" Milo is right, then, in turning Yossarian's accusation around: "'Yossarian, what am I going to do with so much cotton? It's all your fault for letting me buy it.'" It *is* Yossarian's "fault," in the sense that his failure to stop Milo from buying the cotton, which results from his failure to see the potential ramifications of Milo's purchase, leads to the death of Mudd. Unless we wish to argue, as Milo does, that the Americans would have bombed the bridge anyway and the Germans would have defended it anyway and, by implication, Mudd would have been killed anyway, we are forced to acknowledge Yossarian's contribution, albeit indirect and involuntary, to the tragedy at Orvieto.

Yossarian's relation to Doc Daneeka's death is more obvious. It is Yossarian "who made it possible for Dan Daneeka to collect his flight pay each month without ever climbing back into the womb [i.e., an airplane]. Yossarian would persuade McWatt to enter Doc Daneeka's name on his flight log for training missions or trips to Rome." Without this arrangement, of course, Doc would not have been assumed dead when McWatt crashed his plane: "The first person in the squadron to find out that Doc Daneeka was dead was Sergeant Towser, who had been informed earlier by the man in the control tower that Doc Daneeka's name was down as a passenger on the pilot's manifest McWatt had filed before taking off."

Yossarian's part in the deaths of Kid Sampson and McWatt is also hinted at. Although McWatt had buzzed the wooden raft long before he killed Kid Sampson, the implication in the following passage is that he began to do so more frequently after Yossarian convinced him not to buzz his tent any more: "McWatt was incorrigible, and, while he never buzzed Yossarian's tent again, he never missed an opportunity to buzz the beach and roar like a fierce and low-flying thunderbolt over the raft in the water." In an earlier passage we are told that he "flew his plane as low as he dared over Yossarian's tent as often as he could, just to see how much it would frighten him, and loved to go buzzing with a wild, close roar over the wooden raft floating on empty oil drums." After he no longer flies over Yossarian's tent "as often as he could," McWatt "never missed an opportunity" to buzz the beach and the raft, thus immensely increasing the chances of an accident like the one which actually occurs when his plane dips suddenly and chops Kid Sampson in half.

Finally, and perhaps most important, Yossarian is to blame for Nately's death. Heller plants and nurtures this idea, first, by having Nately's whore attack Yossarian immediately after she learns of her lover's fate, second, by having Yossarian swear "that Nately's death had not been his fault" and say, "'What do you want from me? . . . I didn't kill him,'" third, by making Nately's whore ubiquitous once she starts trying to kill Yossarian, and fourth, by letting Yossarian offer several unsatisfactory explanations of her behavior: "'She never did like me. Maybe it's because I broke his nose, or maybe it's because I was the only one in sight she could hate when she got the news'"; "Yossarian thought he knew why Nately's whore held him responsible for Nately's death and wanted to kill him. Why the hell shouldn't she? It was a man's world, and she and everyone younger had every right to blame him and everyone older for every unnatural tragedy that befell them." The inadequacy of these reasons is obvious, since each explains only the whore's initial reaction, not her fanatic international pursuit of Yossarian that presumably extends beyond the final pages of the novel. But the conspicuous lack of any better explanation forces us to supply our own. The only possibility is that Nately's whore knows intuitively what Yossarian has not yet learned, that he is to blame for Nately's death, not in an impersonal way, but in a way that justifies her behavior toward him personally.

In an enigmatic passage, the narrator apparently places blame explicitly on Yossarian for Nately's death: "In a way it was all Yossarian's fault, for if he had not moved the bomb line during the Big Siege of Bologna, Major —— de Coverley might still be around to save him, and if he had not stocked the enlisted men's apartments with girls who had no other place to live, Nately might never have fallen in love with his whore." The first and second parts of this sentence appear to be causally related, when in fact they are not, at least not on a literal level. After Yossarian moved the bomb line, Major —— de Coverley had flown to Florence, but it was in Rome that Nately had found his whore, several months *before* the Big Siege of Bologna. Literally speaking, Yossarian cannot be at fault, even indirectly, for Nately falling in love with his whore. Therefore, Yossarian cannot be considered the catalyst for Nately's decision to fly more missions so he could continue courting his whore after he had finished his tour of duty. Yet the narrator seems to imply in this passage that Yossarian *is* to blame ("in a way") for Nately meeting the whore, the first link in the chain that leads to his death. "It was all Yossarian's fault," the structure of the passage seems to say, because he moved the bomb line, which made Major —— de Coverley fly to Florence and stock the enlisted men's apartments (in Rome) with girls, including the whore Nately meets and falls in love with, then refuses to leave behind when he finishes his 70 missions. Significantly, it is on Nately's 71st mission that he is killed; if he had not wanted to stay and court his whore, he would never have flown his fatal mission.

Yossarian can also be blamed in more tangible ways for Nately's death. First, his refusal to sanction Dobbs's plot to murder Cathcart after the missions have been raised to 60 means that Cathcart is around to raise the missions to 80, guaranteeing that Nately flies his 71st, on which, ironically, Dobbs is killed, too. Second, Yossarian does not have the courage to kill Cathcart himself when Dobbs refuses to go along with him. Third, as we have seen, Yossarian can be blamed for the deaths of Kid Sampson, McWatt, and Doc Daneeka, which make Colonel Cathcart so upset that he raises the missions to 70. And, fourth, Yossarian's decision to ask Milo for help in stopping Nately from flying more missions leads to Milo's discussion with Cathcart in which Cathcart realizes Milo's indispensability and Nately's availability ("'Yes, Nately will fly more.'") and decides to raise the number of missions to 80.

There is yet another way that Yossarian is personally responsible for Nately's death and for the deaths of all the other men in his squadron—including Clevinger and Snowden—who die during a mission. In a word, Yossarian is guilty of complicity. His essential sin is in lending his presence and his tacit sanction to the system perpetrated by the USAF and distorted by Cathcart and Korn. By not deserting and by continuing to fly missions, his feeble protests against bureaucracy are worse than useless because they not only do not stop anyone from getting killed but they engender further tragedy. The chaplain is brutally interrogated because Yossarian, out of boredom and impatience with red tape, had signed the name A. T. Tappmann to a letter he was censoring. Worse yet, Yossarian's refusal to wear his uniform after Avignon and his threat to cause trouble about the number of missions only makes Colonel Cathcart more nervous and insecure and therefore more willing to raise the missions again, "the most tangible achievement he had going for him."

Perhaps the most telling case, though, is Yossarian's most daring and most futile exploit of silent rebellion—the moving of the bomb line during the great Big Siege of Bologna, which serves only to delay the inevitable and to get rid of Major —— de Coverley, the one person on Pianosa capable of cutting through the red tape and ending Cathcart's tyranny. When the narrator tells us, "In a way it was all Yossarian's fault, for if he had not moved the bomb line during the Big Siege of Bologna, Major —— de Coverley might still be around to save him," the implication is clear—he might still be around to save all of them from the spiraling missions requirement and from the grasp of Catch-22 itself.

Major —— de Coverley's ability to sweep away the horrors and absurdities of military life is firmly established in the scene describing his return to the base during the Glorious Loyalty Oath Crusade. His power over the other officers, including Colonels Cathcart and Korn, is established several times, as in the following passage: "so many other people treated Major —— de Coverley with such profound and fearful veneration that Colonel Cathcart had a hunch they might all know something. Major —— de Coverley was an ominous, incomprehensible presence who kept him on edge and of whom even Colonel Korn tended to be wary. Everyone was afraid of him and no one knew why." His very name is indicative of his awe-inspiring qualities: "No one even knew Major —— de Coverley's first name, because no one had ever had the temerity to ask him."

In "real" life, of course, it would be true that all the men who continued to fly their missions could be considered partners in evil as much as Yossarian, but the structure of the novel places the fictional burden almost entirely on him. He can be held personally responsible for virtually everything in the book: "In a way it was all Yossarian's fault." This is true, first, because he—far more than any other single character—is intimately related to every significant event in the novel, either as a primary cause (e.g., with Kraft's death), as a secondary cause (e.g., with Mudd's death), as a catalyst (e.g., with the fight in the officers' club), or as a participant (e.g., with Snowden's death). Secondly, of all the characters in the book, Yossarian is the only one flying missions (i.e., going along with the system) who fully understands the absurdity, the danger, and the evil of doing so. His complicity, therefore, is the most obvious and the most hypocritical. Thirdly, of all the characters in the book, Yossarian has the most charisma, so his complicity is the most influential: Milo, Dobbs, the chaplain, and Doc Daneeka seek him out for advice and sympathy; Orr works for months to make the tent livable for him; Clevinger tries desperately to find holes in his argument; Chief White Halfoat won't drive until he's sure Yossarian is in his jeep; Hungry Joe spends most of his time with Yossarian, hoping to photograph him sexually engaged with some girl; McWatt buzzes Yossarian's tent and nobody else's; the "last person in the squadron Major Major wanted to be brought down with a flying tackle by was Yossarian"; and Colonel Cathcart turns "white as a sheet" upon hearing his name.

Finally, the enormous success of Yossarian's refusal to fly more missions further emphasizes his powerful influence over the affairs on Pianosa and his blameworthiness for not trying such a ploy earlier, before all his pals were killed. Even Havermeyer and Appleby, his least friendly acquaintances, come to ask questions and offer encouragement when Yossarian begins to walk backwards with his gun on his hip and refuses to fly more missions. In addition, "people kept popping up at him out of the darkness to ask him how he was doing. . . . People in the squadron he barely knew popped into sight out of nowhere as he passed and asked him how he was doing. Even men from other squadrons came one by one to conceal themselves in the darkness and pop out. . . . Even one of his roommates popped out to ask him how he was doing and pleaded with him not to tell any of his other roommates he had popped out." Significantly, the narrator uses the same phrase to indicate his success that he had used earlier to describe his bungling: "The men with seventy missions were starting to grumble because they had to fly eighty and there was a danger some of them might put on guns and begin walking around backward too. Morale was deteriorating and *it was all Yossarian's fault*" (italics added). Later, Heller has Colonel Korn drive the point home: "'The men were perfectly content to fly as many missions as we asked as long as they thought they had no alternative. Now you've given them hope, and they're unhappy. So the blame is all yours.'"

Clearly, of all the people on Pianosa after Major —— de Coverley's disappearance, Yossarian had the best chance of destroying, or at least undermining, the mechanism by which men were being killed every day, for Cathcart and Korn rather than for their country. The fact that he does not use his leverage fully until the end of the novel suggests that he, rather than Milo or Wintergreen, is the real culprit of *Catch-22* and that, at its most basic level, Heller's work is the story of Yossarian's education in power and responsibility. By making everything in the novel, the good as well as the evil, Yossarian's "fault," Heller argues that the individual, not bureaucracy or the establishment, still holds the final trump.

CLINTON S. BURHANS JR.

Spindrift and the Sea:
Structural Patterns and Unifying Elements in Catch-22

If my experience is at all representative, a particular and unusual danger lurks in the serious study of this work. Inevitably, there comes a time when, looking around at accumulations of notes, charts, and commentaries, you suddenly bust out laughing at yourself in an unexpected illumination of your own absurdity in taking the thing so seriously. In that strange flash of disorientation, you feel like one of Heller's characters, like maybe a bookkeeper for Milo Minderbinder.

Fortunately, this fit of sudden sanity dissolves, as it rightly should; for the comic anarchy which provokes it is only the surface of *Catch-22*, not its sustaining structure. Critics have consistently been challenged by the question of the work's structure and unity and with various and conflicting results. In the main, such discussions center around two viewpoints: some critics argue that the work is episodic and formless; others find it organized according to some particular principle or method. Neither position, it seems to me, need necessarily, nor in fact does, exclude the other. The narrative surface is obviously episodic and apparently chaotic; but this surface formlessness is central to the novel's thematic experience, and it rises from strong and multi-level structural patterns and a variety of unifying devices.

Seeking these patterns and devices in *Catch-22* involves a long and often frustrating analysis, beginning with an elusive sense of underlying

From *Twentieth Century Literature* 19, no. 4. © 1973 IHC Press of Immaculate Heart College.

structure and unity and ending with that sense becoming conviction amidst an overwhelming mass of supporting information. Despite the constant episodic zigzags which comprise *Catch-22*'s narrative surface, the novel is built on a central conflict, two sub-plots, and a host of motifs. What Heller has done is to break up the logical and chronological development of these narrative elements by taking bits and pieces of all three and mixing them together with dashes of expository and rhetorical comment without regard to logical or temporal or spatial connection. The result is an apparent—but only apparent—jumble of comment, character, and event consistent with contemporary esthetic tendencies away from reason, time, and space as ordering categories.

Nevertheless, a basic structure can be discovered holding the novel subtly together. This structure can best be visualized as a kind of narrative tree, with the trunk comprised primarily of the main plot (Yossarian's efforts to get off flying status either by achieving the required number of missions or by having himself declared insane) and two sub-plots (the struggle between Peckem and Dreedle for command of the Wing, and Milo's syndicate). Around this trunk grow in abundance two kinds of branches, arranged for visual convenience one on either side. Those on the left, whether simple references or detailed episodes, are expository flashbacks made once for information purposes or repeated for thematic effect. Those on the right are a different kind of flashback, one which I have not encountered elsewhere. The best way to describe them, I think, is to call them foreshadowing flashbacks; that is, again whether simple reference or detailed episode, most of them after the first add links in a chain of information drawn out and completed at some length. Thereafter, references to these subjects become conventional flashbacks repeated for thematic effect. The result is the paradox of suspense through flashbacks; and, I think, as this paradox suggests, an ingenious fusion of time planes into the simultaneity of existential time, a fusion entirely consistent with what seems to me the fundamental existential theme of the work.

Visualizing this narrative tree and looking down it, one discovers that Heller has done something in each chapter to link it to the preceding chapter—a continuing action or condition, references to time or to historical events, mention of the number of missions required or flown. Sometimes these links are slight and tenuous, as in Chapters Six, Eight and Twenty-four; they may appear at the beginning or be buried in the middle or only surface in the end; still, they are usually there, and they do function, if only subliminally, to tie the narrative together.

Amplifying this masked but functional narrative continuity, *Catch-22* develops in a five-part alternating structure. The trunk of the narrative tree bends twice, breaking its straight line into three sections and two substantial bulges. The first part, through Chapter Ten, establishes and develops the narrative present; that is, each chapter, however fragmented in time or place, event or character, does something to maintain and advance the narrative present and its problems established in the opening chapters. The second part flashes back to the Great Big Siege of Bologna in Chapters Eleven through Sixteen; and a third part returns to the narrative present as in the first part in Chapters Seventeen to Twenty-two. Another long flashback, this time to Milo Minderbinder's operations and to the origins and growth of his M & M Enterprises, forms a fragmentary but essentially sustained fourth part in Chapters Twenty-two through Twenty-four. A fifth part returns again to the narrative present in Chapter Twenty-five and remains there with increasingly less fragmentation to the end.

That these structural sections are neither arbitrary nor accidental is suggested by the clearly transitional chapters with which Heller surrounds the two major flashbacks. Chapter Ten ends by introducing the Great Big Siege of Bologna; and Chapter Seventeen opens shortly after the two Bologna missions by returning Yossarian to the hospital at the time of Chapter One and ends with Yossarian out of the hospital again and coming to Doc Daneeka a second time for aid after Major Major had refused to help him in Chapter Nine. Similarly, Chapter Twenty-two introduces the earlier trip to Cairo on which Milo had tried to corner Egyptian cotton; and Chapter Twenty-five refers both to the Chaplain's seeing a naked man in a tree at Snowden's funeral—the episode which ends Chapter Twenty-four—and to his continuing efforts in the narrative present to help Yossarian and the other men by trying to get the required number of missions reduced.

Despite *Catch-22*'s many and sudden shifts in scene, episode, character, motif, and time, then, the narrative trunk makes it clear that Heller has distributed sufficient elements of continuity and transition to give the work a controlling structural design beneath its kaleidoscopic surface. However much this narrative surface may disguise it, *Catch-22* is built on a five-part alternating structure in which sections developing the central conflict and sub-plots in the narrative present (parts one, three, and five) alternate with long flashback sections providing additional background and exposition and also functioning to fuse the work's time planes (parts two and four).

Another glance down the narrative tree suggests a second structural pattern, a tonal structure. Beginning with the end of Chapter Twenty-nine and Chapter Thirty and culminating in Chapter Thirty-nine, the novel darkens measurably into almost insupportable horror. The crucial episode is the mission against the undefended mountain village, a totally unnecessary mission in which poor people unconnected with the war are to be killed without warning for publicity photos of tight bomb patterns. The tonal shift in this episode is clear and sharp. Earlier episodes focus on individual combatants as voluntary or involuntary participants in a familiar if horrifying and ridiculous game with ultimate consequences, like the descriptions of Yossarian's experiences on missions; or on perils and death remote in time, like the Ferrara mission; or on horrors contained within farcical situations, like Milo's bombing of the squadron. Such episodes reflect real horrors but to some degree, at least, cushion the reader against experiencing them, insulate their effects on him. Not so with the mission against the mountain village. It is immediate; it is probable; it is barren of justification; it is stark murder; it is unspeakable outrage; it is uncushioned horror. Even Dunbar, who has up to this point looked primarily after himself and sought only to lengthen his life span by taking no unnecessary risks whatever, rises in protest, denounces the mission, and risks court-martial by intentionally missing the village.

The tonal shirt I am suggesting here is indicated in several other ways as well. Four of the novel's five basic structural sections and the beginning of the fifth precede the mission to the mountain village; no basic structural change follows it. Clearly, something different is going on in this final third of the novel from the structural alternation of the first two-thirds: something more focused, more concentrated, more intense. Similarly, most of the novel's riotous fragmentation of time, place, character, and event occurs in its first two-thirds: most of the flashbacks, for example, appear in these chapters. The ratio is around four or five to one, not only in number but also in the variety of their subjects, again suggesting a more intense focus in the novel's final third on the narrative present and its immediate problems. Finally, despite the long months of peril, neither Yossarian nor any of his friends, the central characters in the novel, die before the mission to the mountain village. But one by one they die or disappear thereafter, like lights going out in a gathering darkness.

A three-part tonal structure, then, seems evident. The first part, Chapters One through Twenty-nine, establishes the tone by which the novel is usually characterized: a predominantly and broadly humorous tone, a mixed tone in which fear and desperation are contained within and controlled by exploding jokes, gags, puns, parodies, and satiric attacks, the tone of a fireworks display in a thunderstorm. The second part, Chapters Twenty-nine through Thirty-nine, pivoting on the mission to the mountain village, shifts to a much different and more consistent tone, one of deepening despair whose growing darkness envelops the humor and turns it increasingly sick and savage. The third part, the last three chapters, shifts again to another mingled tone, one of resigned desperation broken by revelation and release.

Within these general structural patterns of organization and tone, *Catch-22*'s central conflict develops in a conventional plot and sub-plot structure. The central conflict is, of course, Yossarian's struggle to survive the war either by flying the required number of missions or by getting himself removed from combat status. In each purpose, he finds himself constantly blocked: Col. Cathcart keeps raising the required number, and the military system functions by insuperable devices for keeping Yossarian on combat status. The resulting conflict develops in a generally classical pattern: exposition, initiation, complication, rising tension, crisis, and climax moving in the main chronologically and climactically within a welter of expository and foreshadowing flashbacks and providing points of departure for a host of related puns, jokes, parodies, and satiric attacks.

Catch-22 begins *in medias res* with Yossarian in full and close pursuit of the magic number: 45 missions are required, and he has flown 44. In Chapter Two, Col. Cathcart raises the number to 50 and in Chapter Six, when Yossarian has 48, to 55. In Chapters Nine and Seventeen, Yossarian has reached 51, but in Chapter Nineteen, the magic number rises to 60. By chapter Twenty-eight, Yossarian is once more closing in; but Cathcart raises the ante again, to 65 in Chapter 30 and to 70 in Chapter 31. In Chapter Thirty-five, Cathcart raises to 80; and Yossarian, after reaching 71, decides in Chapter Thirty-eight to end this exercise in futility and fly no more.

Flashbacks provide additional information on Yossarian's efforts to gain this elusive military brass ring. Chapter Six returns to the previous Fall when 25 missions were required and Yossarian reached 23 by flying six missions in six days. At that point, Col. Cathcart became the new group commander and raised the number to 30 in celebration. By the time of the Orvieto mission the following Spring, 35 missions were required (Chapter Ten); and after the two Bologna missions, when Yossarian had 32, the number increased to 40 (Chapter Sixteen). In Chapter Seventeen, Yossarian reached 38, and Cathcart raised again to the 45 required in Chapter One.

A similar pattern emerges from the second aspect of Yossarian's struggle to survive: his efforts to get off combat status. After leaving the hospital in Chapter One, he tries unsuccessfully to persuade Doc Daneeka to help him (Chapters Four and Five) and considers refusing to fly any more missions (Chapter Six). He decides to go to Major Major; and when he refuses to help (Chapters Seven and Nine), Yossarian tries Doc Daneeka again (Chapter Seventeen). He asks the Chaplain for help, and the Chaplain responds vigorously but without result (Chapters Nineteen, Twenty, Twenty-five). After Yossarian is wounded over Leghorn, the psychiatrist at the hospital certifies him insane but confuses him with another patient, who gets sent home instead of Yossarian; and he tries Doc Daneeka again (Chapter

Twenty-Seven). In Chapter Thirty-eight, he refuses to fly any more missions; and after recognizing that he cannot go through with his deal with Cartcart and Korn (Chapters Forty and Forty-one), he deserts.

Here, too, flashbacks fill in important background material. In Chapter Ten, Yossarian decides not to fly the first Bologna mission; and in Chapter Fourteen, he aborts by forcing Kid Sampson to turn back. On the Avignon mission, he is smeared with Snowden's blood and viscera and refuses to wear a uniform again (Chapter Twenty-four). And a final flashback revealing the full import of Snowden's secret reveals as well the deepest motivation of Yossarian's struggles (Chapter Forty-one).

Like the structural and tonal patterns, then, this two-pronged central conflict functions coherently at the heart of *Catch-22*, though it is not always immediately or continuously available. In less detailed and more fragmentary form, two sub-plots work similarly within the apparent welter of the novel's surface. The lesser of these is the contest between Generals Peckem and Dreedle for command of the Wing. The background and opening moves of this contest are suggested in Chapter Three, and Peckem's aims and campaign appear in Chapters Twelve and Nineteen. General Dreedle's position and ultimate defeat are indicated in Chapter Twenty-one, and Scheisskopf joins Peckem and learns of his real war in Chapter Twenty-nine. In Chapter Thirty-six, Peckem replaces Dreedle, only to discover that his command is now under the broader jurisdiction of the newly promoted Scheisskopf (Chapters Thirty-seven and Forty).

A more fully developed sub-plot describes the rise of Milo Minderbinder from new mess officer to business manager of the whole war as head of M & M Enterprises. As with Yossarian, Milo's story begins *in medias res*. Chapters Two, Seven, and Nine reveal his extravagant and luxurious mess-hall operations in full bloom; and flashbacks in Chapters Ten, Twelve, and Thirteen explain how Milo became a mess officer and describe some of the operations of M & M Enterprises. Syndicate operations and Milo's spreading influence and power appear in Chapters Nineteen, Twenty-one, and Twenty-two; and Chapter Twenty-four is a flashback to the beginnings of M & M Enterprises and its major operations. Chapters Twenty-eight, Thirty-five, Thirty-nine, Forty-one, and Forty-two reflect further glimpses of Milo's gourmet mess halls and his increasingly ubiquitous syndicate. In Chapter Forty-two, Col. Cathcart and ex-P.F.C. Wintergreen have joined Milo; and he is well on his way not only to controlling the war but also to owning the world by giving everyone a share in it.

As the narrative tree suggests, then, the episodic and fragmented narrative surface of *Catch-22* masks and is sustained by a complex and multi-dimensional structural design compounded of an alternating five-part basic structure, a three-part tonal structure, and a conventional plot and sub-plot structure. Moreover, this complex structural design is reinforced by several unifying devices: chronology, recurring characters, and a variety of motifs. The result is paradox: structure and unity sustaining and controlling episodic chaos.

However much the narrative surface may obscure it, the events of *Catch-22* are chronologically related. Heller refers to several specific dates and occasions and to historical events, and these can be supplemented by time references and cross-references in the text. We know, for example, that it is late August when the Chaplain talks to Col. Cathcart about lowering the missions from the new number of 60 and that this conversation occurs at least several weeks after Yossarian leaves the hospital at the beginning of the story. We also know, from a reference to his rest leaves in Rome, that Yossarian leaves the hospital and returns to his tent at least several weeks after the fall of Rome on June 6, 1944. We can thus infer that the narrative present at the beginning of the story is sometime in July, 1944. When Yossarian returns from the hospital at that time, he learns that Col. Cathcart has raised the required missions to 50; and a short time later, probably in middle or late July, he raises the number to 55. At this point, Yossarian recalls the death of Mudd "three months earlier"; therefore, since Mudd died on the Orvieto mission, we can date that mission as sometime in April, 1944.

By thus using firm dates and events as constant reference points and by cross-checking against them and against each other the main episodes of the novel, it is possible to organize an occasionally loose but generally reliable chronology for *Catch-22*:

1941:	Yossarian in Army—qualifies for transfer to Air Cadet training
1941-1943:	Yossarian an Air Cadet at Santa Ana, California, and Lowery Field, Colorado—Grand Conspiracy of Lowery Field
NOVEMBER 26, 1941:	Yossarian in hospital at Lowery Field
NOVEMBER 26, 1942:	Yossarian in hotel room with Mrs. Scheisskopf
1943:	Yossarian goes overseas via Puerto Rico—Splendid Atabrine Insurrection
SEPTEMBER, 1943:	Required missions at 25. Yossarian flies his 23rd, to Arezzo—Col. Nevers killed—time of Salerno beachhead—missions raised to 30
APRIL, 1944:	Beginning of M & M Enterprises—Orvieto

	mission—death of Mudd
MAY, 1944:	Required missions at 35
	Development of M & M Enterprises—Milo tries to corner Egyptian cotton Ferrara mission—deaths of Kraft and Coombs—first soap poisoning of mess
	Milo bombs squadron
	General Peckem schemes to take over combat command
	Great Big Siege of Bologna—second soap poisoning of mess—Yossarian's 32nd mission—missions raised to 40
	Yossarian goes into hospital
JUNE, 1944:	Yossarian leaves hospital, flies six more missions—time of fall of Rome
	Yossarian and Orr on leave trip with Milo Avignon mission—death of Snowden
	Yossarian naked in tree at Snowden's funeral
	Yossarian naked at decoration for bravery in Ferrara mission
	Clevinger disappears in cloud
JULY, 1944:	Missions raised to 45—Yossarian has 38, goes into hospital again—time of beginning of book
	Yossarian leaves hospital—missions raised to 50
AUGUST, 1944:	Yossarian flies four more missions—missions raised to 55
	Yossarian flies 51st mission
	Yossarian tries to punch Col. Cathcart in Officer's Club
	Missions raised to 60; Paris liberated (August 25, 1944)
	General Peckem gaining in struggle with General Dreedle
SEPTEMBER, 1944:	Yossarian wounded over Leghorn—goes into hospital again—Americans pushing into Germany, 8th Army takes Rimini, Gothic Line collapsing
	Yossarian returned to combat status—flies two more missions—second Avignon mission—Orr shot down again
	Third Bologna mission—Orr shot down and disappears

	Scheisskopf joins General Peckem's command
	Raid on small Italian mountain village—Germans above Florence
	Deaths of Kid Sampson and McWatt—missions raised to 65
OCTOBER, 1944:	Missions raised to 70
	Yossarian gets new roommates—two months after invasion of Southern France (August 15, 1944)
NOVEMBER, 1944:	Yossarian breaks Nately's nose on Thanksgiving Day—goes into hospital to see Nately—Dunbar to be disappeared
	Yossarian has 70 missions—Chief White Halfoat dies
DECEMBER, 1944:	Missions raised to 80—Dobbs and Nately killed on La Spezia mission
	General Peckem becomes wing commander—under General Scheisskopf
	Yossarian has 71 missions, refuses to fly any more—Dunbar and Major Major disappear
	Yossarian knifed by Nately's whore—goes back into hospital
	Hungry Joe dies
	Col. Cathcart and Ex-P.F.C. Wintergreen partners in M & M Enterprises
	Yossarian deserts—Germans driving towards Antwerp in Battle of Bulge

Despite the general consistency of this chronology, Heller occasionally errs in computation. For one, it seems unlikely that Cathcart would increase the required number of missions only by ten in the seven or eight months between September, 1943, and May, 1944; and it seems even more unlikely that Yossarian would fly only nine missions in the same period—especially after flying six missions in six days in September. The relationship between the number required and the number Yossarian flies is consistent, but the totals are implausible. For another, Heller says at one point that Milo bombed the squadron "seven months" after the period in which Yossarian was an air cadet at Lowery Field in Colorado. But Milo formed his syndicate after April, 1944, and Yossarian had already flown 23 missions seven months earlier in September, 1943. Clearly, then, Heller is off here by a year or two. Again, Captain Black's Glorious Loyalty Oath Crusade is ended by Maj. —— de Coverley when he returns to the squadron from Rome shortly after the fall of the city in July, 1944. But Captain Black began his Crusade when Major Major was made squadron commander instead of him, and Major Major was already squadron commander when Yossarian joined the squadron some time before September, 1943.

Such errors raise some interesting problems. To begin with, they are few and relatively insignificant when measured against the number of events and their generally consistent chronological relationship. Moreover, Heller occasionally makes almost offhand expository comments which indicate that he does have a clear chronology in mind. In describing Yossarian's and Hungry Joe's missions in September, 1943, for example, he concludes with the observation that shipping orders could have saved Hungry Joe "seven days earlier and five times since." At that time, 25 missions were required; and Col. Cathcart, until late in the story, raises the ante by fives. "Five times" would put the number at 50—which is precisely the number required in the narrative present from which Heller is writing at this point.

It is tempting, therefore, to argue that Heller's errors are intentional, that he means them to disguise his general chronological consistency or to contribute to the fusing of time planes which, it seems to me, is an essential element in his thematic purposes. On the other hand and more likely, I believe, they could be the results of simple carelessness. Either way, such errors are insufficient to destroy the basic and generally consistent chronology or to prevent its functioning as a unifying element in the matrix of the story.

Another unifying element is Heller's use of recurring characters. Counting the characters in *Catch-22* poses the same problem as counting them in Chaucer's "Prologue": the sum depends on those you decide *not* to count. The full total of all the characters in *Catch-22* would number armies and hosts; but if the count is restricted to those who are named or otherwise individualized, the result is some eighty or ninety characters. And if the count is only of those whose recurrence is sufficient in number and in distribution to suggest a unifying effect, the total becomes a manageable but still significantly large twenty-six. Yossarian (40), Cathcart (30), Korn (25), Daneeka (22), Dunbar (22), Hungry Joe (21), McWatt (21), Milo (21), Nately (21), Black (19), Orr (18), Aarfy (17), Chaplain (16), Dreedle (16), Wintergreen (16), Nately's whore (15), Snowden (15), Major Major (14), Appleby (13), Danby (13), Halfoat (13), Peckem (13), Clevinger (12), Dobbs (12), Havermeyer (11), Duckett (10)—each recurs throughout the novel in the number of chapters indicated in the parentheses.

Another interesting and valuable way to assess Heller's use of recurring characters is to note how many of these twenty-six appear or are mentioned in each chapter. Two chapters (Six and Thirty) contain some mention or broader function of eighteen of these twenty-six characters, and only one chapter (Eighteen) has as few as one of them. The average is about fourteen per chapter; only three chapters contain less than five, and only fifteen chapters less than ten characters. Clearly, then, Heller uses recurring characters to further the paradox at the heart of his novel's structure: with so large a number of characters (supplemented by the other sixty or so recurring less frequently) in as many chapters, he can achieve a turbulent variety in any single chapter while evoking a subtle sense of unity between the chapters.

Even more interesting and effective, it seems to me, is Heller's use of motifs as unifying elements. Two motif patterns function throughout *Catch-22*: general and climactic. By general motif I mean simply the conventional repetition of concept, theme, image, or event for thematic or stylistic or structural effect; and at least eight such general motifs recur in *Catch-22*: death (36), insanity (30), Yossarian and death (16), Yossarian and sex (14), disappearance (12), Yossarian and hospitals (11), Catch-22 (9) and Washington Irving signatures (7).

Here, again, as with the recurring characters, I have listed the motifs in the order of the number of chapters in which they are at least mentioned. Moreover, these motifs are distributed throughout the novel; and they reflect intriguing thematic suggestions. Supporting and illuminating the earlier discussion of the novel's central conflict, these motifs emphasize that death and insanity characterize the world of *Catch-22*, a closed-system world of sudden disappearance in which hospitals and bizarre behavior are Yossarian's only refuge, and sex and the life-force it represents his true rebellions.

More dramatic and much more complicated are the novel's climactic motifs, by which I mean essentially what I outlined earlier in discussing Heller's use of foreshadowing flashbacks—that is, a progressive repetition in which successive occurrences provide additional details up to a climactic point at which the motif is completed or its full significance revealed. At least six such climactic motifs recur in *Catch-22*: Nately and his whore (17), Avignon and the death of Snowden (14), Ferrara and the deaths of Kraft and Coombs (12), Orvieto and the death of Mudd (10), Orr's whore, stove and ditching (9), and Milo's bombing of the squadron (7).

Clearly, these motifs are closely related thematically to the general motifs and with them to the central conflict: if the general motifs shade in the conditions of the world in which Yossarian struggles to survive and the means which he employs in his struggles, the climactic motifs highlight the principal events and persons through which he comes to know the real nature of his world and his dire need to contend with it. Furthermore, these climactic motifs function even more carefully and effectively than the general motifs as unifying elements. Each one begins early in the novel; with one exception, each develops through a wider range of chapters; and, again with one exception, each one ends its development in a late chapter. Like the general motifs, then, these climactic motifs recur with sufficient frequency and distribution to work as unifying elements; but they contribute even more valuably to this end both in their function as foreshadowing flashbacks and also in the overlapping pattern of their development.

No one or two of these structural and unifying elements would do much to support or control the apparent episodic chaos of *Catch-22*. But, taken together, the narrative links between chapters, the multi-dimensional structural design, the disguised but generally consistent chronology, the recurring characters, and the two kinds of motifs form a surprising and impressive foundation of structure and unity beneath the shifting shapes and colors of the novel's narrative surface.

Despite its occasional flaws, Heller's artistry in *Catch-22* is both more effective and also more impressive than is sometimes granted. Moreover, this artistry is thematically significant. Its combination of formal elements working subtly within and sustaining an obvious surface formlessness argues strongly that the novel's bombardment of jokes and its satiric barrage are equally linked and that both derive from a shaping thematic concern at its core. The sea, too, has its spindrift; but the spindrift is not the sea.

DAVID H. RICHTER

The Achievement of Shape in the Twentieth-Century Fable: Joseph Heller's Catch-22

My title for this chapter implies—states outright, rather—that *Catch-22* not only has a definable shape but that its form represents an achievement towards which contemporary rhetorical fiction had been groping. Whatever might be thought of such a view today, it would have seemed outrageous to most of Heller's early reviewers, who were repelled by the novel's seeming disorganization. The reviewer for the *New York Times* called Heller the Jackson Pollack of fiction, "a brilliant painter who decides to throw all the ideas in his sketchbooks onto one canvas, relying on their charm and shock to compensate for the lack of design. . . . The book is an emotional hodge-podge; no mood is sustained long enough to register for more than a chapter." The *New Yorker* found Heller's techniques symptomatic of a childish mind, one who "wallows in his own laughter and finally drowns in it. What remains is a debris of sour jokes, stage anger, dirty words, synthetic looniness, and the sort of antic behavior . . . children fall into when they know they are losing our attention." Despite its treatment by the critics, *Catch-22* acquired many staunch supporters, particularly in the colleges, where the novel became the object of cult study. By 1967 its popularity, especially in academic circles, was so great that Jan Solomon could write: "Arrived, admired and analyzed, *Catch-22* is now something of an institution; there are no more comments on it

From *Fable's End: Completeness and Closure in Rhetorical Fiction.* © 1974 by the University of Chicago Press.

formlessness. The novel has been accepted as some sort of gifted example of what in literature must be thought to approximate the drip-and-smear school of modern painting." The tenor of Solomon's article, like that of the spate of criticism on *Catch-22* that has come out in the last five years, is that the novel is not in fact formless, that its madness is under tight control (most of the time, that is), and that the principles of its shape yield to analysis. All this is quite correct. The problem with many of the analyses of this work (a few of which we shall be discussing in some detail later on) is that they concern themselves with Heller's techniques in isolation from the ends for which he developed and used them. As a result we have tended to see *Catch-22* as a queer, surrealistic sort of represented action, queer in that Heller seems to pay little attention to temporal sequence and naturalistic probability, perhaps doubly queer in that Heller will frequently hold whatever narrative lines we can follow in abeyance without having considerations of suspense in mind. These oddnesses in Heller's novel become more readily understandable when *Catch-22* is seen in relation to the tradition of the rhetorical novel.

How not *to tell the story*

The main story line of *Catch-22*, stripped of its connection with the other structural and textural elements of the novel, is surprisingly simple. The hero, Yossarian, is a bombardier in the Army Air Corps during World War II who competently but unenthusiastically flies his assigned bombing raids until the gruesome death in his plane of a young radio-gunner named Snowden makes him desperate to stay on the ground. The main conflict with Yossarian's desires is generated by his group commander, Colonel Cathcart, who, in order to bring himself to the attention of his superiors and become General Cathcart, refuses to allow the fliers who have served the required tour of duty to go home and instead raises the number of missions the men in *his* group must serve to incredible figures. Finally, Yossarian simply refuses to go up in his plane again, and Cathcart, unwilling to dramatize in a court-martial how he had exceeded his orders and driven his men to rebellion, offers to send Yossarian home if only he will undertake public relations work for Cathcart and the Army when he gets back to the States. Yossarian does not want to be court-martialed, but neither does he want to sell out and praise publicly the organization he loathes with all his being; in the novel's last chapter he learns that his former roommate Orr, thought to have been shot down and killed, had been able to paddle his life raft from the Mediterranean all the way to Sweden. Yossarian takes this cue and deserts, hoping to join Orr away from bombing missions and Cathcarts, in that Scandinavian oasis where life is sweet and the women willing.

It would not have been difficult to tell such a story directly, if that had been Heller's intention, but Heller is so far from wanting to tell it that he keeps this narrative line from coming into focus until the last pages of the novel. Instead, the scene is taken over with a host of characters and a skein of subordinate story lines, while the temporal sequence is so jumbled—far more so than *V.*'s—that only elaborate notes and an excellent memory can piece it back into order.

The first chapter typifies Heller's method of obscuring the main narrative line of his novel. During this chapter we learn that our hero's name is Yossarian and that he is a captain in the Air Corps, but as exposition for the main narrative line as described above that doesn't come to much. In fact the term "narrative" itself, implying a chain of events connected by cause and effect, seems to be thoroughly irrelevant here. What we have is not a narrative in that sense at all but a sequence of apparently unconnected comic turns—involving the Texan, Yossarian's ambiguous liver ailment, a fire in the hospital, the soldier in white, Yossarian's adventures in mail censorship, a visit from the chaplain, a discussion of the dying colonel attended by the huge string of specialists (including a cetologist drafted into the Medical Corps by mistake who tries to discuss *Moby Dick* with his patient)—comic turns allied to one another only by the consistency of their absurd tone. The temporal sequence is either jumbled within the chapter or left deliberately vague; not even point of view is consistent: some of the "bits" are narrated using Yossarian as a third-person reflector, but others seem to take place outside his ken. The unity of tone is, in a sense, all the reader gets in the way of structure during the early chapters of the novel; we know who the hero is, and we are witness to a good many happenings—all equally significant or insignificant, depending on one's point of view—but there is nothing that could reasonably be called a plot. Early on we know what is troubling Yossarian (they're trying to kill him), but we are not allowed to develop any sense of what we want for him, much less anything in the way of discrete expectations regarding his fate. Though Heller will later (in his own good time) develop a main narrative line which would seem to lend itself to treatment as a serious action, we are allowed no inkling of this for quite a while. We are instead forced to structure the novel paratactically: the coherence of the events is a matter of thematic repetition. The sequence of "bits," related to one another in nothing save their absurdity, forces us to find the structuring principle in rhetorical statement rather than (as in represented actions) in plot, to generalize a thesis about the absurdity of the world. In the chapters following the first one, the world expands from a military hospital to a wide-angle view of the war, but the sequence of bits continues unaltered, so that Heller gradually convinces us of the absurdity of the war. By a process of induction, of successive approximations, we little by little come to understand Heller's thesis. And it is only after the rhetorical structure of the novel is firmly established, after we have begun to react to each incident as an exemplum and are in no danger of grafting the alien notion of plot onto *Catch-22*, that Heller can bring up the important elements of the main narrative line.

Heller's moral vision

Throughout the first chapter of *Catch-22*, Yossarian wears motley, censoring letters in various arbitrary ways, malingering in the hospital with a fictitious liver complaint, playing practical jokes on the Texan and the chaplain. We are even encouraged to think him thoroughly mad, for in his dialogue with the chaplain he shows the crackpot's conviction that only he is sane while the rest of the world is out of its mind. And, as we soon find out, he may very well be right. For the world outside the hospital is at war, which inverts sane values; in war, as the narrator points out, "men went mad and were rewarded with medals. All over the world, boys on every side of the bomb line were laying down their lives for what they had been told was their country, and no one seemed to mind, least of all the boys." To a man committed to his own survival, such a world is indeed absurd, even insane, while he himself will appear insane to those who believe in the war. Yossarian's idealistic friend Clevinger, who is forever getting people into chop-logic arguments, considers him crazy:

> "I'm not joking," Clevinger persisted.
> "They're trying to kill me," Yossarian told him calmly.
> "No one's trying to kill you," Clevinger cried.
> "Then why are they shooting at me?" Yossarian asked.
> "They're shooting at *everyone*," Clevinger answered.
> "They're trying to kill everyone."
> "And what difference does that make?"

Even Dr. Stubbs—the only reasonably humane physician we meet—considers Yossarian insane, though with a difference:

> "That crazy bastard."
> "He's not so crazy," Dunbar said. "He swears he's not going to fly to Bologna."

"That's just what I mean," Dr. Stubbs answered. "That crazy bastard may be the only sane one left."

Heller undoubtedly runs some risk in presenting his hero as a malingerer, a goof-off, and a philosophical coward, especially since the war against which we see him operating is not an immoral mess like the recent one in Indochina, nor a series of futile and bloody campaigns like Korea, but rather the Last Great War for Humanity, World War II. Heller succeeds by manipulating our sense of perspective: we are never allowed to view the war as a contest of ideologies, as democracy versus fascism, or the free world versus the master race, nor are we allowed to view it even in conventionally nationalistic terms. The author makes it quite clear that the men in Colonel Cathcart's group who fall in battle are sacrificed to nothing higher than Cathcart's ambition.

Even Cathcart, Yossarian's main antagonist, is never seen as a thoroughly worthy villain. Like many of the higher officers, Cathcart is simply a ridiculous stooge, "daring in the administrative stratagems he employed to bring himself to the attention of his superiors and craven in his concern that his schemes might all backfire." Complacent that at thirty-six he is already a full colonel, and dejected that at thirty-six he is still merely a colonel, he is a slave to the army's hierarchical chain of command. It is the system as a whole, rather than his character, that has thus made him what he is, so that we are forced to blame it rather than him. And yet he is capable of sending men up in planes to be shot and killed who were long overdue for rotation back to the States and safety.

Thus the alternatives which face a man in Yossarian's position are few. One can be a knave like Colonel Cathcart or his sarcastic subordinate, Lieutenant-Colonel Korn, at once a pillar and a victim of the army's death-mills, dehumanized—robbed of one's soul—by the motives and responsibilities of command. Or one can be a fool, like Clevinger or Nately, going up on sortie after sortie until finally, inevitably, one simply does not come back; one is dehumanized this way, too, for "the spirit gone, man is garbage." Between the upper and the nether millstones, there is no way to avoid becoming soulless garbage except by getting out; Yossarian's eventual desertion thus becomes the only meaningful and sane form of heroism Heller's world allows.

We cannot, of course, understand all this at the beginning of the novel. Nor are we meant to. Heller first shows us the world of the war as absurd and insane, ridiculous in its queer perversions of normal logic and values. It is only after we have begun to take for granted this apparently comic universe that Heller starts to deepen the mood. Gradually we are shown death, first the deaths of men we have never seen, later the deaths of men we have become acquainted with—Yossarian's friends—and in grimmer and gorier detail. Slowly but inexorably Heller reveals the skull beneath the grinning face of the war, so that what we finally come out with—the thesis that governs Heller's fable—is that beneath the absurdity and insanity of war lies the grim reality of death and dehumanization.

"I see everything twice!"

The method of "successive approximations" by which we come to understand first the absurdity of the universe, then the insanity of war, and finally the horror beneath the surface depends on a technique peculiar to *Catch-22*. Instead of going from incident to new incident, with each successive event darker in tone than the last (the essential technique in, say, Mordecai Richler's *Cocksure*), incidents and situations are repeated, frequently with few factual changes, but with detail added to bring out the grotesque horror that underlies their absurd comedy. The characters and events remain what they were, but more is revealed about them. According to James M. Mellard, the first time through we *see*; later, as the experience is repeated, we *understand*: "Because it raises questions that must be answered, . . . Heller's essentially lyrical method forces the recurring images to accumulate meanings until their full significance, their essence, is finally perceived." It is not, as James L. McDonald thinks (in an article strikingly similar to Mellard's in other respects), simply a matter of Heller manipulating "the characters, events, and situations into elaborate parallels which," through their bumping about together in our minds, help to "illustrate the novel's central themes." There is order and pattern to the way in which Heller manages his repetitive structure.

One simple and relatively unimportant example of this pattern is the "soldier in white," who appears three times in the course of the novel. The first time is in the initial chapter, where he appears, swathed in bandages, with an intravenous input and a catheter output whose bottles are periodically switched. Nurse Cramer takes his temperature, finds that he is dead, and Yossarian and Dunbar accuse the bigoted Texan, jokingly, of having murdered him on account of his race. The second time he shows up is during a repetition of the very same hospital scene with which the novel began. (One can tell that it is the same only by noting that the number of missions Yossarian has to fly—forty-five—is unchanged. The number of missions Cathcart has set for the group is virtually the only "calendar" we are allowed in the book.) This time, though, Dunbar and Yossarian are moved almost to rage by the soldier in white's presence and by the orderly, efficient, and thoroughly nonsensical care he receives. Dunbar frantically asks the Texan whether he perceives any kind of life behind the bandages, while Yossarian gets angry at Nurse Cramer for her grotesque solicitude:

> "How the hell do you know he's even in there?" he asked her.
> "Don't you dare talk to me that way!" she replied indignantly.
> "Well, how do you? You don't even know if it's really him."
> "Who?"
> "Whoever's supposed to be in all those bandages. You might really be weeping for somebody else. How do you know he's even alive?"

> "Maybe there's no one inside," Dunbar suggested helpfully. "Maybe they just sent the bandages here for a joke."
> She stepped away from Dunbar in alarm. "You're crazy," she cried, glancing around imploringly. "You're both crazy."

> "I wonder what he did to deserve it," the warrant officer with malaria and a mosquito bite on his ass lamented after Nurse Cramer had read her thermometer and discovered that the soldier in white was dead.
> "He went to war," the fighter pilot with the golden mustache surmised.
> "We all went to war," Dunbar countered.
> "That's what I mean. . . ."

Here the soldier in white is connected up with the war and his lack of human identity in such a way as to associate the war with dehumanization. The scene is still comic, though in a much grimmer way than before, for there are ominous overtones to the last colloquy, foreshadowing the harvest of corpses that is still to come.

The last time the soldier in white appears (much later—Cathcart now wants seventy missions) there is nearly a riot in the hospital. Dunbar begins screaming eerily, "He's back! He's back!" until the fever-crazed inmates begin to think that some disaster has struck the hospital. Dunbar starts to believe— as before he had jokingly said—that there *is* no one inside the bandages, that the doctors sent the phony patient into the ward in order to mock the airmen's situation. As the panic spreads, the soldier in white begins to take on the tenor of a conspiracy of the doctors against the patients similar to that of the top brass against the ordinary crewmen and officers like Yossarian and his friends:

> "They've stolen him away!" Dunbar shouted. . . . "They just took him away and left those bandages there."
> "Why should they do that?"
> "Why do they do anything?"
>
> "Did anyone see him?" Dunbar demanded with sneering fervor.
> "You saw him, didn't you?" Yossarian said to Nurse Duckett. "Tell Dunbar there's someone inside."
> "Lieutenant Schmulker is inside," Nurse Duckett said. "He's burned all over."
> "Did she see him?"
> "You saw him, didn't you?"
> "The doctor who bandaged him saw him."
> "Go get him, will you? Which doctor was it?"
> Nurse Duckett reacted to the question with a startled gasp. "The doctor isn't even here!" she exclaimed. "The patient was brought to us that way from a field hospital."
> "You see?" cried Nurse Cramer. "There's no one inside!"

And it is immediately after this incident that Dunbar, like the soldier in white, is "disappeared," lost to sight, never found.

Another relatively minor character who is developed in this way is Aarfy—Captain Aardvark—who seems to be merely an extremely conventional ex-fraternity boy who has never quite grown up. His jovial confusion—"'I don't think we're at the target yet. Are we?'"—tends to place him in our good books: he is not manic, like Clevinger, so perhaps he is, like Dunbar, one of the finest, least dedicated men we know. But during the investigation of Yossarian's conduct at the bombing of the bridge at Ferrara, where as lead bombardier he took the entire squadron past the target twice, getting the bridge the second time but killing Kraft and his crew, a sour note is added to Aarfy's thoughtless incompetence: the reason Yossarian was unable to get the bridge the first time around, he says, is that "'I didn't have enough time. My navigator wasn't sure he had the right city.'"

Almost immediately afterwards, Aarfy's thoughtlessness contributes to a nightmarish scene. In the second mission over Bologna, Yossarian's squadron runs into a ferocious barrage of antiaircraft fire. Having dropped his bombs on the ammunition dump, Yossarian looks up to find Aarfy in the bombardier's nose bubble, blocking his escape route in case the plane is hit by antiaircraft fire. So Yossarian is stuck with trying to do two things at once: get Aarfy out of the nose back to his station in the body of the plane, and guide McWatt out of range of the flak. Frantically Yossarian screams orders to McWatt, while at the same time he shouts at Aarfy and pummels him with his fists: all the while Yossarian is bellowing at Aarfy his only response is "'I can't hear you, you'll have to speak louder.'" And Yossarian's fists have as little effect as his words; Aarfy is immovable:

> Punching Aarfy was like sinking his fists into a limp sack of inflated rubber. There was no resistance, no response at all from the soft, insensitive mass, and after a while Yossarian's spirit died and his arms dropped helplessly with exhaustion. He was overcome with a humiliating feeling of impotence and was ready to weep in self-pity.

This scene is replayed once more, later in the novel, when after Yossarian has dropped his bombs on Parma, Aarfy misnavigates the plane over the strongly defended seaport of Leghorn. Another barrage of flak comes up at them and Yossarian is wounded by one of the shots:

> "I lost my balls! Aarfy, I lost my balls!" Aarfy didn't hear, and Yossarian bent forward and tugged at his arm. "Aarfy, help me," he pleaded, almost weeping. "I'm hit! I'm hit!"
> Aarfy turned slowly with a bland, quizzical grin. "What?"
> "I'm hit, Aarfy! Help me!"
> Aarfy grinned again and shrugged amiably. "I can't hear you," he said.
> "Can't you see me?" Yossarian cried incredulously, and he pointed to the deepening pool of blood he felt splashing down all around him and spreading out underneath. "I'm wounded! Help me, for God's sake! Aarfy, help me!"
> "I still can't hear you," Aarfy complained tolerantly. . . . "What did you say?"

Aarfy is not actually deaf, but he might as well be. What he has become by this point in the novel is actually much worse: a soulless *golem* insensitive to the most immediate human considerations, only outwardly human and sociable, his fraternity-boy grin fixed to his face like a mask.

The other side of Aarfy is cued by his hilariously bourgeois attitudes toward sex; he is a consummate killjoy. One of the girls Yossarian's squadron picks up in Rome is a slattern in an orange satin blouse whose prized possession is a ring whose bezel is a pornographic cameo. Aarfy gets the girl, but refuses "'to take advantage of a sweet kid like that.'" At which Yossarian is properly livid:

> "Who said anything about taking advantage of her?" Yossarian railed at him in amazement. "All she wanted to do was get in bed with someone. That's the only thing she kept talking about all night long."
>
> "That's because she was a little mixed up," Aarfy explained. "But I gave her a little talking to and really put some sense into her. . . . I know what kind of girls to prod and what kind of girls not to prod, and I never prod any nice girls. This one was a sweet kid. You could see her family had money. Why, I even got her to throw that ring of hers away right out the car window."

There is low comedy in this, as in Aarfy's repeated asseverations that never in his life has he paid for sex. But after the scene recounted above we find a streak of cruelty—of which Aarfy, of course, is totally unconscious—within his fraternity-produced system of values. When Nately hires his own whore and her two girl friends, Aarfy declines to help him by taking one of the girl friends off Nately's hands ("'Nobody has to pay for it for good old Aarfy. I can get all I want any time I want it.'"), but he has another suggestion:

> "Why don't we keep the three of them here until after the curfew and then threaten to push them out into the street to be arrested unless they give us all their money. We can even threaten to push them out the window. . . . Gee whiz," he defended himself querulously. "Back in school we were always doing things like that, I remember one day we tricked these two dumb highschool girls from town into the fraternity house and made them put out for all the fellows who wanted them by threatening to call up their parents and say they were putting out for us. We kept them trapped in bed there for more than ten hours. We even smacked their faces a little when they started to complain. Then we took away their nickels and dimes and chewing gum and threw them out. Boy, we used to have fun in that fraternity house."

The two sides of Aarfy's nature—the bourgeois fraternity boy given to cruel but childish acts of mischief, and the insensate, inconscient golem— merge in his final appearance at the climax of Yossarian's nightmare odyssey through the dark Roman streets. Searching for sanity where it is not to be found, Yossarian rushes back to the officers' quarters looking for Michaela, the homely farm girl who serves as maid in the apartment building:

> She had sallow skin and myopic eyes, and none of the men had ever slept with her because none of the men had ever wanted to, none but Aarfy, who had raped her once that same evening and had then held her prisoner in a clothes closet for almost two hours with his hand over her mouth until the civilian curfew sirens sounded and it was unlawful for her to be outside.
>
> Then he threw her out the window. Her dead body was still lying on the pavement.

Yossarian is horrified at what Aarfy has done, but Aarfy himself shows no remorse. He had to kill her, after all: you couldn't let her go around saying bad things about airmen, could you? And when Yossarian points to her dead body on the street, Aarfy explains that "'she has no right to be there. . . . It's after curfew.'" Yossarian is overjoyed when he hears police sirens coming closer: perhaps there is justice in the world after all, perhaps the irresponsible eventually have to face up to the evils they cause. The sirens close in, and the military police run up the stairs, but it is Yossarian, not Aarfy, that they arrest—for being in Rome without a pass.

Aarfy is Heller's most literal representation of the kind of dehumanization that the war works on men *while they are still alive*. In the course of the novel, he is revealed as a soulless monster, acting out his cruel fantasies and retreating into the irresponsibilities of his frat-boy smile, knowing that amid the enormities of the war, while thousands of soldiers and civilians are being killed every day, his own tiny murder is but a peccadillo of no importance at all. It is certainly, in the eyes of the men of war, a far more venial crime than Yossarian's, for the latter is a breach of army discipline, a sin against the system, while murder is, after all, the army's business.

It is important to note that the change in Aarfy from the beginning of *Catch-22* to its end does not involve any alteration of his character. We are not left, in other words, with the comforting belief that before he went to war Aarfy was a good man and that he became a rapist and a murderer under the pressure of combat. On the contrary, his character is not so much altered as progressively revealed; the only change, if one can call it that, is that his increased opportunities for noxious mischief lend greater plausibility to that revelation.

A more important character, whose function and development are similar to Aarfy's, is Milo Minderbinder, pilot and war-profiteer. Like Aarfy, he is introduced casually, with a brief reference to the fact that the mess hall runs smoothly in his absence; we take Milo, from the description of Yossarian's gourmet dinner, to be simply one whiz of a mess officer. We soon find out that Milo is also an entrepreneur of the old school, evidenced when he trades McWatt's yellow bedsheet for a package of pitted dates and somehow winds up with both the dates and the bedsheet; Milo's explanation is in a great American tradition:

> "He stole the whole bedsheet and I got it back with the package of pitted dates you invested. That's why the quarter of the bedsheet is yours. You made a handsome return on your investment, particularly since you've gotten back every pitted date you gave me. . . . The remaining quarter of the bedsheet I've set aside for myself as a reward for my enterprise, work, and initiative. It's not for myself, you understand, but for the syndicate. That's something you might do with half the bedsheet. You can leave it in the syndicate and watch it grow."

And it does grow—the syndicate, not the half-bedsheet. Milo sets up an international trading cartel: each bomber group in all the armies (except the Russians—Milo won't trade with Communists) lends him a single plane to deliver groceries in, and Milo uses the huge fleet to cruise about the Mediterranean snapping up bargains, buying low and selling high, and making an enormous profit for himself.

Without seeming to. Yossarian is puzzled by the fact that Milo buys eggs in Malta for seven cents apiece and sells them to the mess halls in Pianosa for only five cents. Yossarian—and we readers—have been wondering about that since page 66, but it is not explained for another one hundred sixty pages how he manages to do it—or why. At last Yossarian asks him why:

> "I do it to make a profit."
>
> "But how can you make a profit? You lose two cents an egg."
>
> "But I make a profit of three and a quarter cents an egg by selling them for four and a quarter cents an egg to the people in Malta I buy them from for seven cents an egg. Of course, *I* don't make the profit. The syndicate makes the profit. And everybody has a share."
>
> ". . . Why don't you sell the eggs directly to you and eliminate the people you buy them from?"
>
> "Because I'm the people I buy them from," Milo explained.

"I make a profit of three and a quarter cents apiece when I sell them to me and a profit of two and three quarter cents apiece when I buy them back from me. That's a total profit of six cents an egg. I lose only two cents an egg when I sell them to the mess halls at five cents apiece, and that's how I can make a profit buying eggs for seven cents apiece and selling them for five cents apiece. I pay only one cent apiece at the hen when I buy them in Sicily."

And everybody has a share. Milo's hilarious business antics reach some sort of apogee when he buys the entire Egyptian cotton crop just for the experience of cornering a market, and too late finds out that there is no market at all for cotton, much less for a year's crop.

It is around this point that the darker side of Milo's business ventures starts to come out. In order to raise some cash for his syndicate operations, he goes into the war business himself, contracting with the Americans to bomb a highway bridge at Orvieto and with the Germans to defend the self-same bridge, all at cost plus six percent, with a merit bonus of a thousand dollars for every plane shot down: since both armies are already present to do the fighting, "in the end Milo realized a fantastic profit from both halves of his project for doing nothing more than signing his name twice." The arrangement was wonderful for everyone—everyone, that is, except a flyer named Mudd, who had no sooner arrived at Yossarian's squadron than he was packed aboard a plane, sent over Orvieto, and shot down with the rest of the crew. Milo denies all responsibility for his death, over Yossarian's furious protests; after all, Milo claims, "'if I can persuade the Germans to pay me a thousand dollars for every plane they shoot down, why shouldn't I take it?'" Yossarian pleads with Milo: there is a war on; Milo is dealing with the enemy; people are dying all around them. But for Milo the Germans are *not* the enemy—the Germans are members in good standing of Milo's cartel; the real enemy, for Milo, is the people who don't pay their bills to the syndicate on time. And in the insane logic of *Catch-22*, Milo's position is irrefutable.

In an effort to recoup his losses on the Egyptian cotton corner, Milo tries a variation on his Orvieto arrangement:

One night, after a sumptuous evening meal, all Milo's fighters and bombers took off, joined in formation directly overhead and began dropping bombs on the group. He had landed another contract with the Germans, this time to bomb his own outfit. . . . Wounded soon lay screaming everywhere. A cluster of fragmentation bombs exploded in the yard of the officer's club and punched jagged holes in the side of the building and in the bellies and backs of a row of lieutenants and captains standing at the bar. They doubled over in agony and dropped. . . .

. . . "Milo, this is Alvin Brown. I've finished dropping my bombs. What should I do now?"

"Strafe," said Milo.

"*Strafe*?" Alvin Brown was shocked.

"We have no choice," Milo informed him resignedly. "It's in the contract."

And both the outcry in the press and the congressional investigation are defused when it is learned what a tremendous profit the entire venture had brought in. And everybody has a share. So Milo goes on and on, more prestigious than ever, buying Egyptian cotton and trying to sell it to the mess halls, covered with chocolate, as a confection.

A revealing conversation takes place shortly thereafter, as Milo observes of the tree he has climbed to be with Yossarian, who is watching Snowden's funeral from a branch, "'This is a pretty good tree.' 'It's the tree of life,' Yossarian answered, . . . 'and of the knowledge of good and evil, too.' Milo squinted closely at the bark and branches. 'No, it isn't,' he replied. 'It's a chestnut tree. I ought to know. I sell chestnuts.'" This is emblematic of Milo's outlook on life: the knowledge of good and evil might as well not exist. Milo, like Aarfy, is one of the irresponsibles whose values produce the needless cruelty of war. Neither is a villain in the usual sense of the word; neither actively wills the suffering and death he causes. They are simply moral imbeciles, unconscious of any ethical dimension to their actions. Furthermore, both of them, despite their military dress, represent in exaggerated form civilian attitudes typical of businessmen and young middle-class climbers, and as such they extend the absurdity and horror of *Catch-22* well beyond the war which is its ostensible subject.

We are thus allowed to view Heller's thesis in potentially broader terms than the novel as a whole develops. Milo's cartel is not simply American: M & M Enterprises includes all of Europe as well. And we are explicitly told that the end of the war will not mean the end for Milo. M & M Enterprises, with Milo at its head, will go on, absorbing or merging with its competitors (like ex-Pfc. Wintergreen's rival operation), and staffed with former officers, including the abominable Cathcart, whose executive talents insure their welcome. The world of Catch-22, in other words, will be brought back home, so that returning to the States will in reality be no escape. These peripheral matters become crucial when Heller is arranging his denouement.

Milo's last appearance, like Aarfy's, comes in the "Eternal City" chapter, in which all the varieties of human misery are served up to us at once. Yossarian is looking for Nately's whore's kid sister, the little girl who represents for him the injured innocent of the world. Yossarian goes to Milo, who has power everywhere, and promises to become a good team-player again, to stop rocking the boat by embarrassing Colonel Cathcart with his refusal to fly more missions—if only Milo will use his clout to help him find the girl. They drive to the police station, where Milo reveals Yossarian's problem. The police chief would like to help, he says, but that night he has no manpower: "'Tonight all my men are busy trying to break up the traffic in illegal tobacco.'" All at once Milo forgets about Yossarian and the kid sister while the profit motive wells up in him. As he thinks about the money he can make smuggling tobacco, he turns into a fevered automaton, dehumanized himself just as his arrangements with the Germans had dehumanized Mudd and the other fallen airmen:

> "Illegal tobacco," Milo explained to him with a look of epileptic lust, struggling doggedly to get by. "Let me go. I've got to smuggle illegal tobacco."
>
> "Stay here and help me find her," pleaded Yossarian. "You can smuggle illegal tobacco tomorrow."
>
> But Milo was deaf and kept pushing forward, nonviolently but irresistibly, sweating, his eyes, as though he were in the grip of a blind fixation, burning feverishly, and his twitching mouth slavering. He moaned calmly as though in remote, instinctive distress and kept repeating, "Illegal tobacco, illegal tobacco."

The fascinating thing about both Milo and Aarfy is that, horrifying as they are, they are treated comically throughout *Catch-22*. Perhaps this is possible because they are mechanical versions of men—and the mechanical taking over the human is, according to Bergson, the root source of all humor. But at the same time they represent the spiritual death at the heart of Heller's absurd universe. Heller's economy is such, indeed, that his characters are not a compound of funny and of horrible traits; rather the same characteristic—their dehumanization, their spiritual death—make Aarfy and Milo both comic and horrifying at once.

The soldier in white, Aarfy, Milo: three symbolic characters whose development contributes not only to the texture of *Catch-22* but to its structure as well. Indeed, the opposition is a false one, because in this particular novel structure and texture are one. The structure is a peculiar one, with an element of strict order and an element of apparent randomness. The novel consists of a skein of interweaving threads each developing a single character, symbol, or recurrent action. Within each thread a strict order among the episodes is observed, an order of more and more explicit revelation of the horror inherent in the comic. In symbolic terms, x_1 must precede x_2, x_2 must precede x_3, and so on; and the same would be true of the sequence y_1, y_2, $y_3 \ldots y_n$, and all the other sequences. But the interweaving of the threads is not determined by any such mechanical law: if y_1 immediately follows x_1 early in the novel, there is not guarantee that y_2 will immediately follow x_2: other episodes may be interposed between them, or they may even come in opposite order; furthermore, each thread may have a different number of total episodes, may begin much earlier or much later than other threads. This apparent randomness accounts for the fact that each episode comes upon us as a surprise—there is no predicting when Aarfy, Milo, Hungry Joe will pop up in our field of vision. It is also responsible in large part for the reviewers' accusations that *Catch-22* was the fictional equivalent of an action painting. But the randomness is only apparent: while there is no *mechanical* order observed among the various threads, the skein maintains a remarkable consistency of tone for all its myriad inconsistencies: the degree of darkening of tone alters smoothly, accelerating as we reach the climax in "The Eternal City" and "Snowden." It may well be possible to switch the order of adjacent chapters with little noticeable effect; as the distance between the switched chapters is increased, however, the effect becomes progressively more destructive to the novel's power.

The two most important components of the skein have not been discussed in detail as yet; their especial importance is in the high degree of integration with the main narrative line. Unlike the three discussed earlier, neither is a character: one is a symbol, the other a recurrent action.

Only one catch

The title of Heller's novel is *Catch-22*, and that little phrase, like the characters we have already discussed, is developed through incremental repetitions until its full meaning is understood. The first reference, in Heller's usual practice, tells us little. As Yossarian is censoring letters in the hospital, the narrator reminds us—almost as though it were something that *we* had forgotten—that "Catch-22 required that each censored letter bear the censoring officer's name." Except for the fact of the title and epigraph, we should hardly notice the reference to Catch-22: perhaps it is some clause in the army's regulations. We first begin to understand the elusive power of Catch-22 at the second reference, when Yossarian comes to Doc Daneeka asking to be grounded for medical reasons: he is crazy, he says, and therefore exempt from combat duty. But Doc Daneeka isn't having any—you can't, after all, let crazy people decide whether they're crazy or not—so Yossarian tries a different tack, concentrating on his equally mad tentmate Orr:

> "Is Orr crazy?"
> "He sure is," Doc Daneeka said.
> "Can you ground him?"
> "I sure can. But first he has to ask me. That's part of the rule."
> "Then why doesn't he ask you to?"
> "Because he's crazy," Doc Daneeka said. "He has to be crazy to keep flying combat missions after all the close calls he's had. Sure, I can ground Orr. But first he has to ask me to."
> "That's all he has to do to be grounded?"
> "That's all. Let him ask me."
> "And then you can ground him?" Yossarian asked.
> "No. Then I can't ground him."
> "You mean there's a catch?"
> "Sure there's a catch," Doc Daneeka replied. "Catch-22."
> Anyone who wants to get out of combat duty isn't really crazy."

Some catch, that Catch-22. Orr would have to be crazy to fly another bombing mission, and since he is crazy he doesn't have to. But if he refuses, he is showing concern for his own survival, characteristic of a rational mentality; therefore he is sane, and has to fly. Catch-22 is one of those perverse paradoxes of two-valued logic that delighted Lewis Carroll; it becomes, at this point, symbolic of the absurdity of wartime regulations and of the general insanity of the war Heller's characters are fighting.

We lose sight of Catch-22 for a while, but when Heller picks it up once more a touch of cruelty has been added to its absurdity. The next reference is during Captain Black's Glorious Loyalty Oath Crusade, a project anachronistically reminiscent of the McCarthy era. Black has convinced Milo not to let the men eat until they sign an oath pledging their loyalty to the United States government, all the men except Major Major Major Major, whom Black will not allow to sign loyalty oaths—or eat—because he considers him a Communist:

> "What makes you so sure Major Major is a Communist?"
> "You never heard him denying it until we began accusing him, did you? And you don't see him signing any of our loyalty oaths."
> "You aren't letting him sign any."

"Of course not," Captain Black explained. "That would defeat the whole purpose of our crusade."

And Captain Black's logic in starving Major Major is above reproach: as he himself says, "'It's just like Catch-22. Don't you get it? You're not against Catch-22, are you?'" Catch-22 is thus extended to cover the insane persecutions—the witch hunts—by which good men are ruined.

But we do not find out the whole truth about Catch-22 until the "Eternal City" chapter, when Yossarian, looking for Nately's whore's kid sister at the bordello where she and Nately's whore lived, finds the place empty except for an old cleaning woman, who tells Yossarian that the girls have all been chased into the street:

> "Chased away by who? Who did it?"
> "The mean tall soldiers with the hard white hats and clubs. And by our *carabinieri*. They came with their clubs and chased them away. They would not even let them take their coats. The poor things. They just chased them away into the cold. . . ."
> "There must have been a reason," Yossarian persisted, pounding his fist into his hand. "They couldn't just barge in here and chase everyone out."
> "No reason," wailed the old woman. "No reason."
> "What right did they have?"
> "Catch-22."
> "*What*?" Yossarian froze in his tracks with fear and alarm and felt his whole body begin to tingle. "*What* did you say?"
> "Catch-22," the old woman repeated, rocking her head up and down. "Catch-22 says they have a right to do anything we can't stop them from doing. . . . All they kept saying was 'Catch-22, Catch-22.' What does it mean, Catch-22? What is Catch-22?"
> "Didn't they show it to you?" Yossarian demanded, stamping about in anger and distress. "Didn't you even make them read it?"
> "They don't have to show us Catch-22," the old woman answered. "The law says they don't have to."
> "What law says they don't have to?"
> "Catch-22."

Catch-22 is thus no longer merely a symbol for the absurdity of war. While it is no less insane in its workings than before, Catch-22 has come to include the horror of naked power unchained, the evils that man inflicts on his fellow man in the name of irresponsible authority. And as its essence is inexorably revealed we come to understand the thesis of Heller's novel, that the insanity, the absurdity, the perverse logic of war is only a surface phenomenon, and that beneath that surface lies the horror of death and dehumanization.

But this is not the last reference to Catch-22. It is mentioned just once more, as the "catch" behind Colonel Cathcart's offer to send Yossarian home. Catch-22 dictates Yossarian's part of the bargain: in exchange for release from combat duty and rotation back to the States, Lieutenant-Colonel Korn tells Yossarian that he has to "'like us. Join us. Be our pal. . . . Become one of the boys.'" There, in Cathcart's sunlit office, away from the horrors of the dark Roman streets, it would seem easy to forget about what has just happened, to join forces with the servants and victims of Catch-22, which kills spiritually what it does not deprive of physical life. And Yossarian is indeed tempted: Heller cites Yossarian's close shave when he is offered the opportunity to sell out as an indication of his vital humanity. But he eventually decides not to accept the spiritual death which the deal involves: Yossarian's desertion to Sweden is a decision to put himself, if possible, beyond the reach of Catch-22.

Snowden's death

In chapter 40 ("Catch-22"), Yossarian has tentatively accepted Cathcart's deal; at the very opening of chapter 42 ("Yossarian"), he tells Major Danby, the confused ex-college professor, that he has decided to reject it. No process of reasoning has intervened, nor has Yossarian met anyone with new ideas or new information. But Yossarian has learned something that changes his view of the deal: he—and we readers—have come to understand Snowden's secret.

Snowden is introduced early in the novel, in the question Yossarian asks everyone "that had no answer: 'Where are the Snowdens of yesteryear?'" The flip parody of François Villon hides more intensity than it seems to, for Yossarian "was ready to pursue" the corporal to whom the question is put "through all the words in the world to wring the knowledge from him if he could." But Yossarian's desperation goes almost wholly unexplained; all we can learn now is that "Snowden had been killed over Avignon when Dobbs went crazy in mid-air and seized the controls from Huple."

As the novel progresses, Snowden's death is referred to again and again, always portentously, as though its freight of meaning were too great to be discharged at once. Almost immediately after the first reference, Yossarian brings into his memory Dobbs "weeping pathetically for help," calling for first aid for the bombardier; when Yossarian radios back that he himself is all right, Dobbs keeps begging, "'then help him, help him. . . .' And Snowden lay dying in back." Somewhat later, when Yossarian is in the hospital, we find out something new, that Snowden had a secret which he had "spilled" to Yossarian before he had frozen to death in the back of his plane. And almost immediately thereafter Yossarian gives his version of Snowden's secret: "That was the secret Snowden had spilled to him on the mission to Avignon—they were out to get him; and Snowden had spilled it all over the back of the plane." But Yossarian has always known that everybody is out to get him: this is *not* Snowden's secret (although, in a way, it is part of it), and Snowden's death keeps intruding like an unanswered question as the book continues. We continue to find out new details: that Yossarian refuses to wear his uniform after the Avignon mission, and receives his Distinguished Flying Cross standing naked in the ranks; that it was Dobbs's incompetent flying that had caused Snowden's death; that even the cagy and coy Doc Daneeka showed "glum and profound and introverted grief . . . when Yossarian climbed down the few steps of his plane naked, in a state of utter shock, with Snowden smeared abundantly all over his bare heels and toes, knees, arms and fingers." The references to Snowden—there are more than a dozen of them—become short scenes, connecting up the details more and more coherently and still referring enigmatically to Snowden's "eternal, immutable secret." But it is not until chapter 41 ("Snowden") that the significance of his death is fully understood.

By chapter 41 we have seen death in many forms, heard how Mudd, Kraft, Colonel Nevers and Major Duluth—all people we never meet—have been shot out of the sky; we have heard that Clevinger flew into a little white cloud, never to fly out again; we have seen Kid Sampson cut in half grotesquely by McWatt's propeller, and McWatt himself suicidally fly into a mountain; we know that Hungry Joe was found suffocated with a cat on his face and that Chief White Halfoat died of pneumonia—deaths they themselves had predicted; we have heard how Orr was lost (as we still think) and how Dunbar was "disappeared" by order of the high command; that Dobbs collided with Nately in the air and that both crews were killed. Dozens of deaths have been reported—and yet the phenomenon is still a mystery, unknown to us emotionally at least. This is thoroughly intentional on Heller's part: though he lets the weight of the numbers of the dead oppress us, he interposes his ironic point of view between us and the final vision of mortality, describing Kid Sampson's death as comic Grand Guignol, and reporting the death of Nately—the idealistic kid for whom we have been made to feel fond affection—as simply as he possibly could: "And Nately, in the other plane, was killed too." Heller thus saves until the climactic spot in his novel the revelation of the horror of death and dehumanization, and here

Yossarian's recurrent nightmare is played out in full dress.

The scene begins in the by now familiar manner: the screaming dive, the sound of antiaircraft shells exploding near the plane, and Dobbs begging for help, which Yossarian crawls back into the body of the plane to administer. He finds Snowden with an enormous wound in his thigh, panics at first, then settles down to stop the flow of blood, administer antibiotics (there is no morphine—just aspirin and a note from Milo, whose cartel has taken over the opiates), and bandage the wound. He sits back at last with a sigh of relief, knowing that Snowden will survive, when all at once he notices "a strangely colored stain seeping through the coveralls just above the armhole of Snowden's flak suit":

> Yossarian felt his heart stop, then pound so violently he found it difficult to breathe. Snowden was wounded inside his flak suit. Yossarian ripped open the snaps of Snowden's flak suit and heard himself scream wildly as Snowden's insides slithered down to the floor in a soggy pile and just kept dripping out. A chunk of flak more than three inches big had shot into his other side just underneath the arm and blasted all the way through, drawing whole mottled quarts of Snowden along with it through the gigantic hole in his ribs it made as it blasted out. Yossarian screamed a second time and squeezed both hands over his eyes. His teeth were chattering in horror. He forced himself to look again. Here was God's plenty, all right, he thought bitterly as he stared—liver, lungs, kidneys, ribs, stomach and bits of the stewed tomatoes Snowden had eaten that day for lunch. Yossarian hated stewed tomatoes and turned away dizzily and began to vomit, clutching his burning throat. The tail gunner woke up while Yossarian was vomiting, saw him, and fainted again. Yossarian was limp with exhaustion, pain, and despair when he finished. He turned back weakly to Snowden, whose breath had grown paler. He wondered how in the world to begin to save him.

This is the reality behind the absurd business of war, and now we know it. And yet Heller does not let out all his stops in this scene: he continues, even here, to distract us with "bits" from earlier sections of the novel, like the note from Milo put in place of the morphine, "What's good for M & M Enterprises is good for the country." Phrases like "whole mottled quarts of Snowden" and "Yossarian hated stewed tomatoes" are inserted to forestall the potential sense of climax. For the true climax of the scene is to come not with the revelation of Snowden's death-wound but with the "spilling" of his secret promised since early in the novel. And it is with this—not the gore—that the frisson of recognition comes, for it is here that our emotional reactions are subordinated to, converted into the knowledge that Heller wishes to convey:

> Yossarian was cold . . . and shivering uncontrollably. He felt goose pimples clacking all over him as he gazed down despondently at the grim secret Snowden had spilled all over the messy floor. It was easy to read the message in his entrails. Man was matter, that was Snowden's secret. Drop him out a window and he'll fall. Set fire to him and he'll burn. Bury him and he'll rot, like other kinds of garbage. The spirit gone, man is garbage. That was Snowden's secret. Ripeness was all.

The spirit gone, man is garbage. And whatever eliminates that spirit—physical death, moral death—turns man into garbage. Fear of the former had kept Yossarian from going up in his plane, made him refuse to fly more missions. And it is fear of the latter—spiritual death through moral surrender—that forces Yossarian to reject Cathcart's deal. For it does not matter whether one is shot to death or dehumanized through becoming a servant of Catch-22: garbage is garbage

Sweden and sanity

The conclusion of *Catch-22* is basically a debate, in dialogue form, on the merits of Yossarian's decision not to accept the colonels' deal. Yossarian is not unwilling to be sent home, but it must be on his terms, not theirs: as he himself demands, "Let them send me home because I flew more than fifty missions"—by this time Yossarian has actually flown seventy—"and not because I was stabbed by that girl, or because I've turned into such a stubborn son of a bitch." But that is past praying for: if Yossarian rejects the deal and still refuses to fly more missions, Cathcart will court-martial him on trumped-up charges, suborning witnesses (including Aarfy) to testify against him under the justification that getting rid of Yossarian would be "for the good of the country." Worse still, the servants of Catch-22 have closed their ranks, and Yossarian will no longer be able to play off Milo against Cathcart, or ex-Pfc. Wintergreen—Milo's competition—against the other two: Cathcart has been made a vice-president of M & M Enterprises, which has recently merged with Wintergreen's operation. But Yossarian keeps the knowledge of Snowden's secret before his eyes:

> "Danby, must I really let them send me home?" Yossarian
> inquired of him seriously.
>
> Major Danby shrugged. "It's a way to save yourself."
>
> "It's a way to lose myself, Danby. You ought to know that."
>
> "You could have lots of things you want."
>
> "I don't want lots of things I want."

It is at this point that the chaplain rushes in bringing news—received God knows how—that Orr, shot down months ago over the Adriatic and never heard from since, had washed ashore in Sweden. Washed ashore, nothing, says Yossarian: Orr planned it that way; he had rehearsed for his escape to Sweden and sanity by getting shot down on every mission he flew. The news of Orr's success restores Yossarian's faith in the possibility of human survival, and he decides to escape to Sweden himself, bringing with him the innocent and defenseless girl he had unsuccessfully sought in the Eternal City—if he can find her. He takes his leave of his friends and sets out for a good place, out of reach of the long arm of Catch-22:

> "Goodbye, Yossarian," the chaplain called. "And good luck.
> I'll stay here and persevere, and we'll meet again when the
> fighting stops."
>
> "So long, Chaplain. Thanks, Danby."
>
> "How do you feel, Yossarian?"
>
> "Fine. No, I'm very frightened."
>
> "That's good," said Major Danby. "It proves you're still
> alive."

The ending of *Catch-22* has been subjected to a good deal of scrutiny, and several critics—a solid majority of those who discuss it at all—find it wanting in either the philosophical or the aesthetic dimension. Occasionally this is done without much regard to internal consistency: one critic, having claimed that "the ending of *Catch-22* is an attempt to focus upon the major topic of the book itself, the question of survival," later states that "Heller's ending adds a new dimension to the novel. However it is sharply inconsistent with the bulk of material presented before the last five pages." One does not know whether Pinsker's objection is to the novelty of the material or to the fact that it still focuses "upon the major topic of the book itself"—whether the ending is too inconsistent or too consistent. Actually I suspect that Pinsker is more troubled by the probability of the ending than with Heller's credentials as a thinker with a unified point of view, for he goes on, "The *deus ex machina* character of Orr's miraculous journey is unacceptable to modern sensibilities which demand a greater sense of 'reality'." It is hard to accept this, however, as legitimate criticism, for Heller's mode of probability, which corresponds to Aristotle's category of the "possible improbable," has been fully consistent throughout the novel: to reject the ending on the grounds that we readers "demand a greater sense of 'reality'," is to reject also the soldier in white, Milo's business deals, the biographies of Chief White Halfoat and Major Major Major Major, Nately's whore's murderous peregrinations—the entire novel, in fact, to a greater or lesser extent.

A more pertinent objection is offered by Vance Ramsey, who notes what he calls a "discursive quality" about the last four chapters of the novel:

> This loss of the dramatic quality at the end of the novel points to an even deeper problem, the change in Yossarian. The first part of his story, his reaction to death and his need to disengage himself from all that threatens him, is made poignantly convincing; the last stage of his development, the decision that there is something greater than survival, is not so convincing. Yossarian's morality in saying "no" to the forces which threaten to take him over is supposed to become a morality of social involvement: he is to go to Sweden to try to do something about all of the horrors he has seen in his last night in Rome.

And Ramsey's objection is echoed in a later biographical and critical article by Richard Lehan and Jerry Patch, who declare that the author finished the novel under pressure of a deadline set by his publishers: "Heller, faced with the task of drawing together his sprawling materials, finally did so, but with an abrupt shift of gears." Lehan and Patch quote with approval Sherman Wincelberg's criticism of the denouement as putting Yossarian into "one of those soul-searching conflicts between conscience and self-interest which used to be so popular on live TV. . . . In contrast to the rest of the book's splendid contempt for such niceties, I find it a little on the square side."

Had Heller initially created Yossarian as an egoist devoid of all conscience, concerned with his own survival to the exclusion of all outside claims, and then had him fly off to Sweden after profound self-examination to do social service, these criticisms would be justified. As it is, they are based on a profound misreading of Yossarian's character and Heller's intentions for him. Yossarian is indeed concerned about his own survival and with the forces that threaten it, but at the same time he is concerned for the survival of his friends, acquaintances, and mere colleagues. It is because of this that he interrogates Milo unmercifully, trying to get him to admit responsibility for the death of Mudd over Orvieto; because of this that he is willing to pursue "through all the words in the world" the answer to his riddle, "where are the Snowdens of yesteryear?"; because of this that he mourns in his own unconventional way when Orr is lost over the Adriatic; because of this that he takes his life in his hands to break the news of Nately's death to the latter's girl friend. And on the other side, there is no indication of any incredible altruism in Yossarian's escape to Sweden—barring his intention to take Nately's whore's kid sister with him. Perhaps Ramsey has been misled by Yossarian's talk of his "responsibilities": "'I'm not running *away* from my responsibilities. I'm running *to* them,'" Yossarian declares at one point. But the context makes it clear that Yossarian's "responsibilities" add up to survival—saving his own life and soul: immediately after the above quotation, Yossarian explains: "'There's nothing negative about running away to save my life. You know who the escapists are, don't you, Danby? Not me and Orr.'" There is indeed a change in Yossarian at the end of the novel, but it is not an inexplicable shift in character and motivation; it is rather that he knows at the end, through his understanding of Snowden's secret, that it would be as fatal for him to accept Cathcart's deal as to fly more missions, that neither is an acceptable alternative. Ramsey even seems to understand this, for he suggests that "it is possible to intellectualize [Heller's] result: if Yossarian were to accept the deal offered to him in order to survive, he might still lose his self to the system." But since Ramsey also considers the Milo Minderbinder story and other portrayals of dehumanization of the living as "excrescences" irrelevant to the main theme of the novel—ignoring half of Heller's thesis by doing so—he does not consider such a reading of *Catch-22*'s denouement "artistically convincing."

It is not clear just what sort of ending would have satisfied Heller's captious critics—they themselves do not presume to suggest alternatives that would have been an improvement. It is clear that there are only a few possibilities: Heller could have killed Yossarian off, or he could have had Yossarian mindlessly accept the colonels' deal, or he could have done neither, but at the same time given us the feeling somehow that, no matter what Yossarian did, he would never, never get outside the reach of Catch-22. Any of these would have provided a sense of closure by settling our curiosity about Yossarian's fate but only the last would have provided a denouement equal in force to the one Heller actually chose; only the last would come as close as Heller's ending to providing a sense of completeness. But it would have been an impossible ending given Heller's character and views: Daniel Rosoff, for thirty-seven years an intimate friend of Heller's, informed Lehan and Patch that "Heller could not have written a different ending, could not have concluded his novel on a note of hopelessness" because of his staunch liberal commitments to human and civil rights.

The only thing which I personally find hard to accept about Heller's conclusion is the notion that any country—Sweden, Switzerland, or Shangri-La—could really be beyond the reach of Catch-22: if Milo's planes trade in Denmark for pastry, could they not get to Stockholm? One can easily see that Heller was caught in a bind here, for to the extent that Sweden is vividly portrayed as an island of sanity, the force of the universal horror of Catch-22 is palliated, and to the extent that it remains a mystery, unexperienced by us—we learn only that the girls are sweet and the people advanced—its credibility as a refuge is undermined. Heller gets around this problem by ending his novel with Yossarian just starting on his way, leaving open the question of what he finds when he gets there—or even whether he makes it. Heller has even stated off the record, in fact, that Yossarian does not make it to Sweden, while in the novel itself Yossarian explicitly defines the value of his desertion as lying in the attempt rather than the fulfillment:

> ". . . I've got to get to Sweden."
> "You'll never make it. It's impossible. It's almost a geographical impossibility to get there from here."
> "Hell, Danby, I know that. But I'll at least be trying."

Yossarian's valuing existence for its own sake, his irrational commitment to the attempt to get to Sweden—even though he knows he will never make it—and his absolute revolt against the absurd values of the army which exalt death: all these call up the image of Camus's rebel. The intellectual connection between Heller and Camus has not, in fact, escaped one of Heller's critics. John W. Hunt, whose "Comic Escape and Anti-Vision" we examined in the last chapter, draws a number of significant parallels between French existentialism and the guiding vision of several contemporary novelists. Of Heller, Hunt writes that, although that author has "no quarrel with Camus," he shows little interest in the metaphysical nature of absurdity. This is perhaps an overstatement: certainly the creation of Dunbar, the Camus hero par excellence, betrays a concern on Heller's part for the more "metaphysical" aspects of existentialism; at times Dunbar's dialogue might be a comic pastiche of *The Myth of Sisyphus*:

> "Do you know how long a year takes when it's going away?" Dunbar repeated to Clevinger. "This long." He snapped his fingers. "A second ago you were stepping into college with your lungs full of fresh air. Today you're an old man."
> "Old?" asked Clevinger with surprise. "What are you talking about?"

"Old."

"I'm not old."

"You're inches away from death every time you go out on a mission. How much older can you be at your age? . . ."

"Well, maybe it is true," Clevinger conceded unwillingly in a subdued tone. "Maybe a long life does have to be filled with many unpleasant conditions if it's to seem long. But in that event, who wants one?"

"I do," Dunbar told him.

"Why?" Clevinger asked.

"What else is there?"

But at the same time Hunt is right in that Heller sees—or at least portrays—the existential revolt of action rather than thought: Meursault's revolt could consist of the realization of his happiness and freedom, but Yossarian cannot succeed if he remains passive. And since Yossarian cannot fly more missions or accept Cathcart's deal—both alternatives being forms of suicide—the surrender to the absurd—the only meaningful revolt he can accomplish on Pianosa is to run away. He need not get anywhere, but he will "at least be trying," and the revolt is what is important, not the final results.

It is not only in Yossarian's activity (so unlike Meursault's passive acceptance of the world about him) that he differs from Camus's rebel; Doctor Rieux, the narrator of Camus's *The Plague*, is as "active" a hero as one could wish, and yet the quality of his revolt is different in kind from Yossarian's and points to a basic incompatibility between Camus's thought and Heller's. In a word, there is for Camus no Sweden: the absurdity of the universe inheres in its nature and in that of man. For Heller, on the other hand, it is man's attitudes and institutions—both susceptible of alteration—which are absurd; thus utopia, no matter how far out of reach, is a meaningful ideal for which man may strive. There is, therefore, a sense in which the absurd is for Heller less a metaphysical commitment than a literary technique. Once used by Camus in exposition of his philosophical ideas, the representation of the divorce between purpose and human need, or acts and ends, or man and fellow man, was available to be used by libertarian progressives like Heller for wholly different ends. The conclusions of the two novels, *The Plague* and *Catch-22*, underline the differences between the ideologies of the two authors: Camus uses his denouement, especially Cottard's murderous explosion and the revelation of the death of Mme Rieux, to establish in the most convincing way that the incident of the plague in Oran is but a symbol of the human condition everywhere, that there is no escape. Heller, on the other hand, uses the very desperation of Yossarian's desertion to underline the difference, immense but bridgeable, between the dehumanizing warfare Yossarian is leaving and the more "advanced" and rewarding life he hopes to find.

GARY W. DAVIS

Catch-22 *and the Language of Discontinuity*

Joseph Heller's *Catch-22*, with its irreverent and bitterly comic description of the last days of World War II, has seemed for many of its readers a frighteningly accurate portrait of the "mentality" behind contemporary social and intellectual institutions. Heller's novel, however, issues more than just a simple challenge to the various commercial, military, and religious organizations which govern the lives of its characters. In the world of *Catch-22*, patients' illnesses always coincide with their doctors' areas of specialization, fliers disrupt political indoctrination sessions with cries of "Who is Spain?" or "When is right?", and Yossarian, the bombardier, must struggle against the "logic" of the Air Corps if he is to continue to survive. Such situations reveal how society's institutions reflect fundamental discontinuities in language, thought, and behavior. More than this, they suggest that at the heart of such dislocations is that problematic and radical discontinuity which has been the subject of so much critical discussion.

The question of discontinuity and what it represents for language (and hence for culture as a whole, as well as for poetry, fiction, and drama) clearly has been an essential part of major transformations within contemporary discourse. Allied on many levels with the general movement away from the artistic endeavors associated with "modernism" and toward those of "post-

From *NOVEL: A Forum on Fiction* 12, no. 1. © 1978 by NOVEL Corp.

modernism," the problem of discontinuity obviously involves more than sweeping changes in the form and style of recent writing. It also is related to those movements which have led much of contemporary thought away from a search for continuities in natural, psychological, or cultural being and toward an acceptance of a discourse which acknowledges linguistic, intellectual, and social discontinuities.

This is evidenced by even the most cursory glance at some of the notions about this question. As various anthologies and symposia have shown, the roots and manifestations of recent conceptions of discontinuity are linked to perspectives ranging from Ernst Cassirer's theory that language is a process of "ever-progressive objectification" to Sartre's portrayal of how "things are divorced from their names," from structuralism's understanding of the essential separation of signifier and signified to Merleau-Ponty's interpretation of language as a labyrinth which can reveal only irreconcilable dualisms. For some (and Sartre's character, Roquentin, would seem an obvious example here) linguistic discontinuity may permit discourse to become so dominant over facticity that authentic action and selfhood can only be restored by a renewed understanding of how "the world of explanations and reasons is not the world of existence." Others, by basing their arguments on Saussure's theory of the arbitrary relation of the signifier and signified, have seen in modern notions of the discontinuity of the linguistic sign the possibility of a new literary culture. Roland Barthes has thus suggested the emergence of a literature which, in its acceptance of language as an arbitrary and self-sustaining system of signs, might lead us to the core of what he calls the "linguistic pact . . . which unites the writer and the other."

Even more illustrative of the direction of some of the transformations in our conceptions of discourse and discontinuity are such recent endeavors as Jacques Derrida's "deconstructions" of phenomenological and structuralist theories of language and Michel Foucault's analysis of how the modern *episteme* came to view writing as a process inhabited only by words and the interval between words. Along these same lines Eugenio Donato, echoing Nietzsche as well as Derrida and Foucault, finds that much of modern thought has come to see language as a discontinuous process of interpretation. This interpretation, Donato writes, "does not shed light on a matter that asks to be interpreted, that offers itself passively to interpretation, but it can only seize violently an interpretation that is already there, one which it must overturn, overthrow, shatter with the blows of a hammer. . . . Interpretation then is nothing but sedimenting one layer of language upon another to produce an illusory depth which gives us the temporary spectacle of things beyond words."

Such conceptions suggest the extent to which the problem of discontinuity has been seen as characteristic of modern discourse, even when that discourse intends the kind of referentiality or "illusory depth" mentioned by Donato. Indeed Geoffrey Hartman implies in a recent essay on Derrida's *Glas* that an awareness of the problematic boundaries between nature and artifice, events and interpretations, and even texts and commentaries has become an inescapable part of our intellectual order. Ultimately we appear to be confronted by a situation in which words seem to refer only to other words, and thoughts, to other thoughts. This seems to be the case whether one turns to the existentialists' demand for a discourse consistent with human freedom and responsibility, to Barthes' interest in how society transforms ideas and themes into the substance of signifying practices, or to Derrida's vision of the freeplay of interpretation.

It is in this regard that the relations between *Catch-22* and the questions posed by the discontinuities of contemporary discourse assume major significance. In response to this sense of linguistic, intellectual, and social discontinuity, Heller, like many other contemporary writers, turns to language itself for a basic model of these disruptions. This enables *Catch-22* to expose fundamental discontinuities in our discourse and our other systems of exchange. The novel's most vital implications for our literature thus lie in the way Heller's demythologizing of discourse relates to Yossarian's quest for survival and to the question of whether it is possible to discover a more meaningful, "continuous" discourse.

Names serve as the most obvious point of departure for this. In elaborate parodies of long-standing notions about the nature of language, names, in *Catch-22*, often fail to "properly" designate a particular object, person, or concept. While continuing to believe in all the myths of a "proper" relation between names and things, Heller's characters often identify an object or person solely on the basis of a name (or even a label or chart) assigned by the most haphazard methods. Names soon come to be accepted as independent "realities" capable of affecting a person's sense of his own experiences or identity. Yossarian, when he usurps someone else's hospital bed, becomes for that time "Warrant Officer Homer Lumley, who felt like vomiting and was covered suddenly with clammy sweat," while Major Major, when he first entered kindergarten, discovered that he was not, as he had been led to believe, "Caleb Major," but "some total stranger named Major Major Major about whom he knew absolutely nothing."

The opening scene of the novel establishes another important aspect of this linguistic discontinuity. Assigned the task of censoring enlisted men's letters, Yossarian transforms the job into a game that involves more than just a simple parody of its own military context:

Death to all modifiers, he declared one day. . . . The next day he made war on articles. He reached a much higher plane of creativity the following day when he blacked out everything but a, an *and* the. *. . . Soon he was proscribing parts of salutations and signatures and leaving the text untouched. . . .*

When he had exhausted all possibilities in the letters, he began attacking the names and addresses on the envelopes, obliterating whole homes and streets, annihilating entire metropolises with careless flicks of the wrist as though he were God. . . .

Writing, here, is an activity discontinuous from anything that might be considered "things themselves." Since what happens within this independent world of words is indistinguishable from what happens in "fact," crossing out a name may, in effect, "obliterate" a place. The same logic lies behind Yossarian's attempt to capture the German artillery batteries at Bologna by simply going to the map and moving the red line that indicates the extent of the Allies' conquests. Once again symbolic forms and expressions have the privileged status usually accorded to "reality." In fact even the Air Corps is briefly convinced that Bologna has been captured.

The process seen in these elementary forms of discourse can serve as a model for other intellectual procedures within *Catch-22*. The clichés and illusions of popular culture, for example, take on much the same status granted to signifiers like maps, charts, and names. With no apparent irony Lieutenant Scheisskopf thinks of his own personal life in terms of the formulae and codes of melodrama: he sees himself as a man "chained to a woman . . . incapable of looking beyond her own dirty, sexual desires to the titanic struggles for the unobtainable in which noble man could become heroically engaged." Elsewhere, the most outrageous fantasies go unchallenged if "verified" by the appropriate forms of the Air Corps' language and logic. Yossarian's joke about the Germans' "Lepage glue gun" (a weapon which "glues a whole formation of planes together in mid-air") takes on the conditions of a "reality" when it is repeated to him by the squadron's intelligence officer. Yossarian's immediate reaction is to cry out, "My God, it's true."

Lieutenant Dunbar's attempts to manipulate time follow the same pattern and lead Yossarian's friend far beyond conventional notions about time's psychological dimensions. "You're inches away from death every time you go on a mission," he tells Clevinger. "How much older can you be at your age? A half minute before that you were stepping into high school, and an unhooked brassière was as close as you ever hoped to get to Paradise. Only a fifth of a second before that you were a small kid with a ten-week summer vacation that lasted a hundred thousand years and still ended too soon." On the basis of such observations Dunbar constructs a private temporal order within which virtually any psychic experience may be granted the status of "reality." The privileged status of this order suggests that, since pleasant experiences make time seem to pass more quickly, the way for him to make his life last as long as possible is to fill it with as many dull, unpleasant, and distasteful conditions as he can.

The Air Corps' manner of operation, in *Catch-22*, reveals that this discontinuity extends into all areas of its behavior. At the insistence of General Peckem the Air Corps has become concerned with making neat "bomb patterns," although, as the General informs Scheisskopf, a bomb pattern is only a phrase "I dreamed up a few weeks ago. It means nothing, but you'd be surprised how rapidly it's caught on." The Army's entire administrative procedure arises from this ability to put purposeless, self-reflexive discourse into action within its field of activity. Ultimately its self-contained organization and action define a closed world whose "illusory depth" becomes its inhabitants' only "reality." Major Major learns this when he discovers that most of the official documents he receives do not "concern him at all. The vast majority consisted of allusions to prior communications which Major Major had never seen or heard of. There was never any need to look them up, for the instructions were invariably to disregard."

As the novel suggests in other scenes, the workings of this language and logic even manage to transform traditional understandings of such concepts as "death," "presence," and "absence." Yossarian's tentmate for much of the time is a "dead man" who had been killed before officially reporting to the squadron. The Army maintains that since the man "had never officially gotten into the squadron, he could never officially be gotten out." Yossarian is told to keep sharing his tent with Mudd's personal belongings and official "presence." If this situation reveals how the discontinuities of knowledge can turn what is generally thought of as death's "absence" into the functional equivalent of "presence," Doc Daneeka's final plight presents a telling reversal of this theme. Listed as part of the crew for McWatt's airplane the day it crashes, the doctor is declared "dead" by the Air Corps, though everyone on Pianosa knows that Daneeka was safely on the ground all the while. His physical appearance never can refute the "facts" of official knowledge. When people begin to act as if he really were dead, Daneeka's "life" is transformed into a functional absence.

These famous examples of the novel's peculiar logic illustrate the extent to which *Catch-22* exposes the meaninglessness of our conventional understanding of discourse and its processes. Indeed the most familiar expression of this logic shows how signifiers, psychological definitions, and knowledge itself are deployed without reference to any "real" human or natural content. "There was," we learn, "only one catch and that was Catch-22, which specified that a concern for one's own safety in the face of dangers that were real and immediate was the process of a rational mind. Orr was crazy and could be grounded. All he had to do was ask; and as soon as he did, he would no longer be crazy and would have to fly more missions." The "elliptical precision" of this logic reveals that the word "crazy" and the question of Orr's sanity are relevant only to whether he flies combat missions or asks to be grounded. Since both actions are functions of the Army's discontinuous rules, sanity and selfhood are now revealed to be elements of a field of play which is as closed as Yossarian's games with the soldiers' letters. Moreover, by showing that Orr's sanity is to be determined solely on the basis of whether he does or does not agree to fly more missions, Catch-22 demands that we think of the self as unrelated moments of discourse rather than as a continuous or creative entity in itself.

From games with the soldiers' correspondence to rules about a flier's sanity, Catch-22 reveals that the men of the Air Corps must now see as arbitrary and perhaps illusory what they previously accepted as "proper" relations between nature and artifice, things and words, or even events and interpretations. At the same time situations like Orr's challenge the conventional assumption that there is any "proper" relation between such entities; indeed Catch-22 exposes our most fundamental myths about both subjectivity and the possibility of perceiving things in themselves. By bringing to the surface the often hidden workings of our language and logic Catch-22 forces us to recognize that "things" are no different than the perplexing appearances typified by the chaplain's "vision" of a naked man in a tree. It simultaneously reveals the "subject" to be only those interplaying levels of "Optical phenomena," *déjà vu*, *jamais vu*, and *presque vu*, which Chaplain Tappman experiences as a "subtle, recurring confusion between illusion and reality . . . characteristic of paramnesia."

Such disruptions of customary understanding demonstrate how Catch-22's victims are severed from what they had thought of as "existence." Abandoned to a labyrinth of words and appearances, they are elements of a discourse which, referring only to itself, neither comprehends nor controls some "world" beyond. As Yossarian comes to understand, it does not matter if Catch-22 actually exists. "What did matter," he discovers, "was that everyone thought it existed." For this reason words spoken to Yossarian while he is still in cadet school, "We're all in this business of illusion together," project the very essence of Catch-22's reasoning.

Significantly Heller sees these linguistic and intellectual discontinuities reflected in our social systems and institutions as well. Milo Minderbinder can buy eggs for seven cents apiece and still make a profit selling them for five cents, while, as the old woman in Rome declares, "Catch-22 says they have a right to do anything we can't stop them from doing." The truly dangerous nature of this discourse is dramatically realized in Colonel Cathcart's attempts to impress his superiors, for his actions and their effects do more than expose the peculiar nature of the language implicit within the most basic concepts of Western philosophy (or even within the idea of "philosophy" itself). Cathcart volunteers his squadron for as many missions as he can, hoping that credit for the men's exploits will result in his own rapid promotion. He therefore sets in motion a grotesque version of Zeno's paradox in which he invariably increases the number of missions the men must complete whenever a flier nears that point at which he can be rotated out of combat duty. Unable to ever finish their combat tours and equally unable to escape from Cathcart's system, the fliers one by one fall victim to German flak and their own commander's zeal for advancement.

As the situation within Cathcart's squadron demonstrates, the Air Corps and its representatives manage to define the "reality" within which their men live simply by setting themselves and their discourse between an individual and any sense he might have of something existing beyond his own words and thoughts. This enables the Army to define the "reality" toward which discourse is directed, regardless of how illusory that "reality" may be or how much these definitions may defy various "normal" conventions. "That's my trouble, you know," Yossarian finally realizes. "Between me and every ideal I always find Scheisskopfs, Peckems, Korns, and Cathcarts. And that sort of changes the ideal." This process allows the Air Corps to blind fliers to what would seem the most obvious situations. Not even Yossarian is able to convince his friends that, as he puts it, "The enemy . . . is anybody who's going to get you killed, no matter *which* side he's on." Heller presents a fitting physical analogue to this general situation in his description of Yossarian's reaction to the compartment which houses the B-25's bombardier. Enclosed within this plexiglass equivalent of the Air Corps' autotelic discourse, Yossarian finds the physical and logical conventions of "normality" significantly inverted. The crawlway leading to an escape hatch now seems only an impediment to escape, while his fellow crewmen have become obstacles to his survival.

On another level this discontinuity is expressed in the activities of Milo and his ubiquitous M & M Enterprises. In a way which underscores the close alliance between conceptions of language, society, and economics within the modern intellectual order, Milo's power is based upon two general assumptions: that everyone agrees to and has a "share" in his syndicate, and that there is, beneath this, some "proper" relation between the shares and a "reality" beyond. These assumptions help Milo create a mercantile empire which, like the capitalist system itself, holds a controlling interest in many of the combatant armies. The very essence of Milo's endeavor, though, exists solely as discourse. The shares are only the "words 'A Share' written on the nearest scrap of paper" and the syndicate's profits always are as fictional as its shares. Much the same discontinuity is embodied in Milo's physical appearance. "Milo's mustache was unfortunate," we find, "because the separated halves never matched. They were like Milo's disunited eyes, which never looked at the same thing at the same time." More important, however, is the way Milo's manipulations of the language of discontinuity allow him to justify economic victimization of friends, contracts to simultaneously attack and defend the German-held bridge at Orvieto, and bargains to bomb and strafe his own squadron.

As Milo and M & M Enterprises remind us, violence and the characters' often unusual attitudes toward violence are inseparable from the question of discontinuity. But, in contrast to the worlds of words and administrative procedures, violence never appears to be neatly confined within the Air Corps or any other military or economic organization. Milo's bizarre business deals have vicious effects on others; civilians like Luciana, the mysterious young woman Yossarian meets in Rome, have their bodies mutilated by the bombs of those who have come to liberate them; and the inept, internal rivalries of the Air Corps cause the needless bombing of undefended villages. In one scene Yossarian discovers that Aarfy, the ambitious, perpetual fraternity boy, has murdered the maid who works in the officers' apartment in Rome:

> Yossarian was aghast. "But you killed her, Aarfy! You killed her!"
> "Oh, I had to do that after I raped her," Aarfy replied in his most condescending manner. "I couldn't very well let her go around saying bad things about us, could I?

Aarfy's explanation is virtually a paradigm of Catch-22's logical procedures and does more than suggest the fallaciousness of certain kinds of "acceptable" acts and rationalizations. It also reminds us that even when the characters' discourse seems clearly exposed as a manipulation of discontinuous symbolic forms, these activities can have violent effects on others. Aarfy's words thus reveal how the closed discourses of Catch-22 permit the novel's characters to ignore both this truth and the actual physical horrors around them. Clevinger thinks that because the enemy indiscriminately shoots at everyone it is not really true that the Germans are trying to kill Yossarian, and Yossarian comes to believe that the hospital, because it makes "a much neater, more orderly job" of death, represents a refuge from the war. Thus when the MPs fail to arrest Aarfy and, instead, seize Yossarian for "being in Rome without a pass," they are simply adhering to one of Catch-22's most deeply rooted processes.

On the other hand all of these situations emphasize the difficulties involved in any attempt to "escape" from either the Army or its closed system of logic. The basic direction, however, that such efforts should take seems indicated in the dénouement of Captain Black's Great Loyalty Oath Crusade. Ignoring the oaths, pledges, and performances of "The Star Spangled Banner" which Black has made prerequisite to even the men's meals, Major —— de Coverly neither argues with Black's system nor tries to outwit it. He simply denies its authority by commanding, "Gimme eat." Heller himself focuses on this question in his interview with *The Realist*. "What distresses me very much," he declares, "is that the ethic which is often dictated by a wartime emergency has a certain justification when the wartime emergency exists, but when this . . . ideology is transplanted to peacetime, then you have this kind of lag which leads not only to absurd situations, but to very tragic situations."

In *Catch-22* concern with such conditions is reflected in the way virtually all social and intellectual institutions, from the Air Corps to the language of philosophy, are transformed into parodies of themselves. This does more than display these institutions' basic irrelevance; it discloses how their intellectual foundations are, and perhaps always have been, obstacles and threats to our survival. "The stimulus for a certain action," Heller asserts in the same interview, "justifies an action. If the stimulus is not there and the action exists anyway, then you've got the right to examine why you're doing it." *Catch-22* as a whole, like the scene involving Michaela's death and Aarfy's attempted explanation, exposes a similar and equally crucial aspect of Catch-22's logic. It unmasks foundations and consequences of that long-standing convention that there is some "proper," even "natural" set of names or metaphors upon which are based our language and knowledge, and to which we appeal for our senses of value and justice. The effect is not simply to reveal the characters' isolation from "reality." It exposes how the problematic nature of language has been obscured within the familiar myths of the "proper" relation between "words" and "things."

It often is contact with some form of violence, rather than an intellectual demystification, which reveals this to Yossarian. This is evident relatively early in the novel, when the bombardier succeeds in avoiding the mission to Bologna. Having used a trivial mechanical failure to relieve his crew from what has been rumored to be the squadron's most dangerous assignment, Yossarian goes to the beach, where, ironically, nature itself appears in the form of a frightening, tumultuous process. Yossarian's walk through the streets of Rome mixes the fantastic and grotesque in a way that further demonstrates to him the distorted violence of experience, the completeness of the physical and spiritual destruction which have been brought about by human imagination and institutions. And near the very end of the novel Yossarian finally sees through all the confusions surrounding Snowden's death to discover in the gaping wound in the radio-gunner's chest the horror of what Snowden has suffered.

Such moments seem to suggest the necessity for some kind of direct encounter with whatever "reality" may or may not lie "outside" discourse. This, superficially at least, would seem to be the "meaning" of Yossarian's experience over Avignon. "Man," he discovers in Snowden's suffering, "is matter," a fragile container for "liver, lungs, kidneys, ribs, stomach and bits of the stewed tomatoes . . . eaten that day for lunch." It is a "message," read quite literally in Snowden's entrails, which reminds us that with the "spirit gone, man is garbage. . . . Ripeness was all." For this reason Yossarian's recurring vision of what happened that day and the refrain, "Where are the Snowdens of yesteryear," which is such an intimate part of that memory, would seem to demand that we demythologize our closed systems of discourse to confront the apparently "existential" verity of our own mortal and material being. This infers the achievement of a discourse free of the discontinuities exemplified by Catch-22. Its speakers would be able to declare, like Dunbar, that it is not really the "quality," but the mere continuation of one's existence that should be treasured. Its "philosophers" would, like the old man in Rome, find civilizations' "ideals" to be clichés which make more sense when their "logical" sequence is inverted than when they are spoken in their conventional manner.

Through much of the novel the institution of some such "proper" discourse, on the social as well as the linguistic and intellectual levels, remains one of the few hopes seemingly open to Heller's characters. But, as Catch-22 exposes from the first, neither an arduous process of linguistic and intellectual purification nor the remnants of some "original" speech from which mankind has fallen can lead us to a "natural" discourse in which "matter" and "language" are bound together by some primal "word." This is the import of the events that take place over Avignon, for the scene is marked by the implication of a language of literary allusion (the overtones of *King Lear* and Villon's "The Ballad of the Dead Ladies"), referentiality (Yossarian's reading of the "message" in the entrails), and even metaphysics (the "spirit" without which man is "garbage") into Yossarian's encounter with the physical horrors of Snowden's death.

The bombardier's seemingly "existential" confrontation with Snowden's innards thus discloses that we can no more dwell within some hypothetical order of simple materiality than we can speak in a language free of the self-reflexive discontinuities which make possible Catch-22 and all its variations. It is a scene, therefore, which exposes how discourse and matter are inextricably entwined in human experience. Experience is not a question of oppositions between "matter" and "symbol," "nature" and "art." It is, instead, a question of how "things" and "events" are inseparable, even indistinguishable from "discourse." But they are not made so by that mythic figure of the "proper word," upon which so much of our economic, social, philosophic, and literary language is believed to be based. Matter and discourse, this scene asserts, are doubled, even reversible functions within a world whose "illusory depth" always has been indistinguishable from whatever we have granted the privileged status of "reality."

This, obviously, is why Heller concludes that it is hopeless to try to either master or reform the discontinuities of discourse. As the fates of Dunbar and the old man in Rome remind us, our ability to manipulate discourse does not lessen our vulnerability to Catch-22 and mortality. Like Yossarian and his friend, Orr, one can only "flee." When, Heller explains, "the monolithic society closes off every conventional area of protest or corrective action," there is no alternative but "flight, a renunciation of that condition, that society, that set of circumstances."

The difficulties which mark Yossarian's desertion at the end of the novel reveal the extent to which even this alternative is involved in the complex question of discontinuity. On one side Yossarian finds the Air Corps, that institution which, on every level, is a parody of the myths which make possible closed, discontinuous discourses of all kinds. Its offer to make Yossarian a returning "hero" exemplifies its fundamental processes. On the other side is Yossarian's vision of Sweden as a place of even more than political refuge and physical safety, a land, he thinks, where "the girls are so sweet" and the "people are so advanced." It is a place whose image as a kind of regained paradise reveals that its bases are, like those of Catch-22 itself, founded on the myths of natural experience and a "proper" metaphoric language as the foundation of value. This forces us to question the nature of that act of desertion which concludes the novel, asking whether it is a genuine movement toward a world of continuous discourse and experience (a declaration that, as always, our only recourse is to the ancient myths of a realm of pure, immediate experience) or a recognition about fiction, as an interplay of levels of discourse, which ties *Catch-22* to recent understandings of discontinuity and to the transition from "modernism" to "post-modernism."

It is in this regard that the significance emerges of the alternatives offered at the novel's conclusion. The world of the Air Corps is one which is closed as well as discontinuous. In contrast Yossarian's image of Sweden, even though it is based upon the same discontinuities as Catch-22 and its manifestations, maintains a fundamental openness which makes it neither as autotelic nor as monolithic as institutions like the Army and M & M Enterprises. Heller himself points to this when, discussing the final scenes of the novel, he declares that he no more thinks of Sweden as a real paradise than he believes that Yossarian ever will get there. Sweden and Yossarian's desertion are only images of a "goal," an "objective" for those who seek to renounce the world of Peckems, Cathcarts, and Scheisskopfs. Within the novel itself this openness is maintained by our awareness that "Sweden" is part of Yossarian's imagination and of the imaginations of all those who seek to escape the discourse of Catch-22. In the way that both the characters and the readers of the novel are kept from forgetting the fundamentally "fictional" nature of this "Sweden" we are all reminded of how the world "beyond" is known only in the form of that "illusory depth" which Donato called "the temporary spectacle of things beyond words." If Yossarian's dream of Sweden seems to hold forth that ancient promise of an attainable "proper" discourse, it does so while still reminding us that it is only a simulacrum of all such dreams; it is a fiction whose essential nature exposes both its own fictionality and the myth of the "word" itself.

Yossarian's choice, at the novel's end, is thus between two kinds of fiction and not between two different worlds or between a fiction and some new reality. One fiction, epitomized by the Army, Milo's capitalism, and the closed language of discontinuity, has lost sight of its own fictionality and has come to believe the myths of its own "proper" bases. The other fiction, "Sweden," exposes its own nature, revealing that it is only an image of our longings for some "refuge" or "home," some "origin" or "center" free of that apparently broken discourse within which mankind inevitably finds itself. This is why the novel's "ending" is so problematic, for it seems to leave open the troubling, vital question of which form of fiction Catch-22 is and what sort of world its hero has chosen. Significantly the novel does not specify whether Yossarian's flight expresses either a preference for the age-old dream of immediate experience or a desire for a discourse of self-reflexively interplaying levels of fiction. Moreover Yossarian's "jump" toward Sweden is taken as much because of his unthinking move away from the descending knife of Nately's whore as it is from any previous decision he may have made. Thus, in much the same way as Yossarian is condemned to remain what Heller calls "a spirit on the loose," forever traversing those invisible yet endlessly marked distances of discourse, the "ending" of the novel is a doubled (non)answer which, like Catch-22 as a whole, forces us, as it forced Yossarian, back into our own fictions and into the experience of fiction itself.

All of this suggests the position *Catch-22* occupies within the development of our recent literature. On the surface its motifs, characters, and situations would seem to suggest that the novel is heir to all the traditions and perspectives which marked the "existential" novel and the problematic legacy of post-Romantic thought. From this point of view *Catch-22* often seems part of that literature's concern with the self's apparently unending struggle to discover and free its own being. It might even be seen as an illustration of how the workings of those principles of discourse embodied in *Catch-22* constitute a violation of humanity's most fundamental nature.

But the fact that the same discontinuity lies at the heart of both what Yossarian flees and what he hopes will be his refuge must remind us, as do the comments of Barthes, Foucault, and Derrida, that the questions raised by linguistic, intellectual, and social discontinuities have become basic to both fiction, as a genre, and to discourse as a whole. In the works of writers like Borges, Nabokov, or Barth (to name just a few) we find more than just depiction of various kinds and forms of discontinuous discourse. We also see fictions which, recognizing and exposing their freedom from the bonds of representation, use discontinuity for their own ends. The Terra and Anti-Terra of Nabokov's *Ada*, the interplaying systems of myth and fiction in Barth's *Chimera*, the strange categories of animal life set forth in Borges' famous Chinese encyclopedia (which Foucault declares gave rise to his own work, *The Order of Things*), all suggest an order of signs in which fiction, free of the burden of some myth of a "proper" correspondence to things, can become an open exploration of discourse itself. Likewise the disruptions of experience and discourse seen in *Catch-22* often foreshadow that other, more radical literature of discontinuity whose violent, "schizophrenic" (as it is often called) freeplay has been associated most frequently with writers like Artaud and Burroughs.

In such works, as in *Catch-22*, fiction becomes a medium which reminds us of our longings for a language of continuity and referentiality at the very same time that it exposes the dangerous, closed discourses to which such desires may lead. Such works inevitably draw us away from systems of "proper" discourse and toward the open interpretation and the interaction of different levels of discourse which are at the essence of the experience of fiction. It is in its revelation of the movement toward such fictional forms and of the epistemic transformations of which they are a part that *Catch-22* has played a major role. Heller's novel exposes, on the most obvious levels, the violent absurdities of our commercial, military, intellectual, and literary institutions. More important is its demonstration that the foundations of these institutions lie in those same recurrent myths of the "word" and of a "proper" metaphoric discourse to which we have turned, so often, as alternatives to the kind of discontinuous languages epitomized by Catch-22. In this way *Catch-22* is part of that reorientation within the intellectual configuration which has led us to begin thinking of writing, not as a system of representation closed by some final "meaning," but as the freeplay of interpretation. Like so much of our recent writing Heller's novel thus demands that we ask whether what we might have thought to be "life" must not also be thought of in terms of a freeplay which is inseparable, even indistinguishable from those processes known as "fiction" and "interpretation."

LEON F. SELTZER

Milo's "Culpable Innocence": Absurdity as Moral Insanity in Catch-22

The label most frequently adopted in describing the themes and methods of Joseph Heller's contemporary classic, *Catch-22*, is without doubt "the absurd." Study after study of this widely discussed novel has at some point resorted to modern notions of absurdity to account for Heller's frankly impossible, yet almost too real, world. This world—specifically, or rather microcosmically, the American Air Force base at Pianosa during World War II—is as much at battle with itself as with anyone else. It is an irrational, sometimes nightmarish world in which one's superior (and even inferior) officers constitute a greater threat to one's life and sanity than the enemy, and where demonstrating one's patriotism may demand not only the signing of interminable and meaningless loyalty oaths, but also the consumption of chocolate-covered cotton. The outrageous senselessness of most of the book's action has prompted several writers to comment on Heller's grotesque presentation of reality and to relate his underlying philosophical perspective to that of Kafka, Sartre, or Camus; or to dramatists working in the "Theater of the Absurd" tradition.

To view *Catch-22* solely in terms of metaphysical chaos, however, is to ignore the novel's heavily satirical thrust, and most commentators have in fact revealed an awareness that the book's concerns are predominantly moral. What has yet to be revealed is how the novel's absurdities—comic and

From *Papers on Language & Literature* 15, no. 3. © 1979 by the Board of Trustees of Southern Illinois University.

otherwise—operate almost always to expose the alarming inhumanities which pollute our political, social, and economic system. That is, what now needs most to be explained is how Heller's wildly unorthodox fictional methods, routinely interpreted as the technical corollary of his absurdist vision, are also the vehicle for his largely traditional, even orthodox, moral satire. This satire can best be seen as a blistering attack on our capitalistic system, a system that has perverted universally accepted ethical norms by unwittingly encouraging the unscrupulous pursuit of wealth and power.

James Nagel—editor of one of the three critical casebooks available on this obviously seminal piece of contemporary fiction—notes in reviewing the immense body of scholarship already surrounding the novel that many critics have viewed "absurdity," "morality," or "sanity" as the book's essential motif. But considering the patently irrational atmosphere of the book, he seems to regard as unlikely the possibility of ever defining these terms adequately. Granted, the action of the narrative does manage to subvert thoroughly the three concepts, but as long as such irrationality is presented from a viewpoint which is itself rational—a perspective detached and judicious—defining "absurdity," "sanity," and "morality" should be feasible enough. The key is to approach the novel's absurdity not in broad metaphysical terms but in specific moral ones, since the book carries its greatest impact at the moral level; and Heller, despite his appreciation of universal chaos, does acknowledge certain ethical norms. The ultimate horror of the phrase "Catch-22," for instance, is felt when Yossarian hears it, as though a knell, from the lips of the miserably bereft old woman in the Roman brothel. And the words are horrible not because they connote a world in chaos but because they indicate that the system controlling the military is morally mad. The horror of such recognition can only be increased once the reader realizes that this insane system rules far more than wartime behavior. Several writers have by now argued that the novel is not basically about World War II at all, and even Heller has pointedly remarked: "I deliberately seeded the book with anachronisms like loyalty oaths, helicopters, IBM machines and agricultural subsidies to create the feeling of American society from the McCarthy period on." Elsewhere the author has expressed his agreement with columnist Murray Kempton's observation that the book's morality is so orthodox as to be "almost medieval," adding reflectively: "I suppose just about everybody accepts certain principles of morality."

What all this is meant to suggest is that the morality which informs *Catch-22* is not problematical but almost commonsensical. Its moral commitments are hardly more difficult to discern than conventional allegory, and it is surely significant that Heller himself has referred to the novel as a combination of allegory and realism—a strong indication that the book's absurdity was conceived from the start as a *moral* absurdity. Moreover, as the title of this article attempts to point out, this absurdity is a product not of immorality but of what might be called "moral insanity": a curiously innocent perversion of reason so total as to blind the actor from any meaningful recognition of the moral components of his (or anybody else's) behavior. The title is also meant to suggest that the book does not revolve around problems relating *either* to absurdity, or morality, or sanity, but to all three of these subjects together, as they form humanity's gravest obstacle to intelligent, scrupulous living, in peace as well as in war. And here once again such an outlook has been anticipated not so much by previous critics as by the author, whose many comments on the novel have provided this study with its strongest extratextual support. In one early interview following the book's publication, Heller described *Catch-22* as "a moral book dealing with man's moral dilemma. People can't distinguish between rational and irrational behavior, between the moral and the immoral. . . . It's insane. . . ."

The novel is, if anything, overloaded with examples of moral and rational disability. Lieutenant Scheisskopf lodges imaginary complaints against Clevinger and then, as a member of his Action Board, simultaneously performs the roles of judge, prosecutor, and defending officer. Colonel Cathcart and Colonel Korn criticize Yossarian for his delinquency in twice flying over a bridge at Ferrara on a single mission, not because the desperately successful maneuver unfortunately cause the death of Kraft and his crew—for such a concern the morally insane Cathcart can see only as "sentimental"—but because it will look "lousy" in the report that must be filed with Headquarters. The solution to the problem is Korn's, and it is perfectly calculated to satisfy the moral insanity of the reigning bureaucracy. In Korn's mind, giving Yossarian a medal might be the wisest thing to do, since "a trick that never seems to fail" is "to act boastfully about something we ought to be ashamed of." And because "it's best to play safe," Korn also convinces Cathcart, his superior officer, to file a request that Yossarian be promoted to captain for his unconventional conduct. The promotion, needless to say, is granted.

Of all the characters exemplifying moral insanity in the novel, by far the most prominent of them is the incredibly manipulative black market entrepreneur Milo Minderbinder, the squadron's mess officer. Despite the overflow of commentary on the novel, no one has provided a thorough analysis of his character or thematic purpose. This is particularly surprising since Heller has described the book as fundamentally not about the second world war but "the contemporary regimented business society"—and Milo is undoubtedly the most striking and significant representative of that society. This is hardly to say that Milo's role has been overlooked, for while critics have generally given him scant attention as compared to Yossarian, the book's hero, they have in most cases identified his narrative function accurately. They have, among other things, appreciated (or rather damned) him as a "caricature of the American businessman," as embodying "the whole mystique of corporation capitalism," as "the mythic hero of organized greed —of unregulated free enterprise," as "capitalist free-enterprise run amok," as "the symbol of American business and western world capitalism," as "a myopic encapsulation of the Madison Avenue mentality," and as representing "untrammeled private enterprise, a utilitarian business ethic, and the entire moral superstructure of American capitalism itself."

If it can be comfortably asserted that *Catch-22* is a novel harshly critical of our controlling institutions and that the book's absurdity is practically indistinguishable from its satire, then Milo—by forming the bull's eye of the author's satirical targets—deserves to be viewed as quite as important as the more sympathetic protagonist, Yossarian. And perhaps one of the crucial ironies of the book is that Milo is in some ways scarcely less sympathetic than his fellow officer. Although Heller's negative estimate of Milo's mercenary character is never really in question, he does take pains—even while attacking him—to create in the reader a certain qualified positive regard for him. When Yossarian looks distrustingly at Milo early in the novel, we are told: "He saw a simple, sincere face that was incapable of subtlety or guile, an honest, frank face . . . the face of a man of hardened integrity." And Milo's "hardened integrity"—however repellent it may finally be—is real enough. He may sell cigarette lighters, as does Ex-P.F.C. Wintergreen, but whereas Wintergreen's lighters are pilfered from the quartermaster, the lighters which Milo offers for sale—though they may have been obtained deviously— are never stolen outright. He may collaborate with the Germans to defend a bridge against an American attack (an attack which, bizarrely, represents a business deal made with American authorities), but the author must still concede that "the arrangements were fair to both sides." And while he is not above bribery if his Enterprises require it, he confides to Yossarian that he cannot feel safe among people who accept bribes, for "they're no better than a bunch of crooks."

As self-serving and hypocritical as Milo's sentiments may be, there is no doubting their sincerity, so that we cannot dismiss as mere sarcasm Heller's description of his eyes as "liquid with integrity" or his face as "artless and uncorrupted." The problem is that such integrity is completely at the service of moral ideals that cannot, in all sanity, be understood as anything but corrupt. As Heller puts it, Milo "could no more consciously violate the moral principles on which his virtue rested than he could transform himself into a despicable toad. One of these moral principles was that it was never a sin to charge as much as the traffic would bear." Another one of Milo's principles is that business contracts must be honored at all costs. And while this may necessitate his purchasing vastly more cotton than he can dispose of (since as a novice in the commodities market he once bought up the entire Egyptian cotton crop), his sacred pledge of allegiance to contracts generally redounds to his fortune—and to the misfortune of everyone else. He defensively argues that the Germans, "members in good standing of the syndicate" over which he presides, are not really enemies, and that he is thus obligated to "respect the sanctity" of his contracts with them. But it is he himself who arranges and mercilessly executes the tremendously profitable deal with the Germans to bomb and strafe his own base. And he is able to commit this cold-blooded atrocity with a clear conscience, for he desperately needs more funds to continue buying all the cotton called for in his other inviolable contract. Human impediments are not merely obscured by his morally insane business ethic—they disappear altogether.

Milo also believes in loyalty to his squadron; and Heller, in his heaviest satirical vein, has him pompously rebuke Yossarian late in the novel for his refusal to fly more missions for the insatiable Cathcart. We are told that Milo "shook his head reproachfully and, with pious lips pursed, informed Yossarian in ecclesiastical tones that he was ashamed of him." Such indignation not only points toward Milo's utter insensitivity to death, but anticipates Yossarian's devastating attack on the military police in Rome four pages later. Inspecting with despair the wanton destruction of the whores' apartment in Rome, Yossarian pictures "the fiery and malicious exhilaration with which they made their wreckage, and their sanctimonious, ruthless sense of right and dedication." Milo's own dedication to his country, however, runs a distant second to his devotion to unbridled private enterprise. He has in fact argued earlier that the squadron should be loyal enough to his syndicate to buy its cotton "till it hurts so that they can keep right on buying my cotton till it hurts them some more"—one more indication that his total absorption with monetary gain has dispossessed him of all empathy. He has firmly convinced himself that for the syndicate's well-being the men should be willing to risk theirs and consume his urgently concocted chocolate-covered cotton—even though, as Yossarian wearily pleads with him, "People can't eat cotton." Heller's absurdist brand of allegory should be clear enough: Milo's ruthlessly capitalistic commitments do not, and cannot, support life.

The syndicate that is M & M Enterprises appears at last to be mostly illusory. Milo may proclaim over and over again that "I don't make the profit. The syndicate makes the profit. And everybody has a share." But inevitably the point must arrive at which everybody's having a share is tantamount to nobody's having a share—nobody, that is, but Milo, who is shown throughout as in complete control of the syndicate's multifarious operations. The myth, or meaninglessness, of well-nigh universal ownership is most pointedly suggested in the scene with the rebelliously skeptical Major from Minnesota, who confronts Milo demanding his share of the syndicate. Milo responds to the challenge "by writing the words 'A Share' on the nearest scrap of paper and handing it away with a virtuous disdain." Milo's self-righteous contempt for the Major suggests in turn that he conceives of business as something like a bond that never reaches—nor is intended to reach—maturity: it exists for its own compulsive sake and all its profits, like interest payments, go directly back into its ever-expanding self. Heller seems to understand keenly the morally vicious cycle that has so often characterized the heartless striving after material riches. Anything derived from such thorough displacement of feeling is more symbolic than real, so that the final taste of success can be no more savory, or sustaining, than Milo's chocolate-covered cotton.

Despite Milo's self-deceiving protestations that "what's good for the syndicate is good for the country"—a deliberate parody of Charles E. Wilson's famous statement about General Motors—Heller unequivocally demonstrates that Milo's syndicate is basically antagonistic toward his country, and that loyalty to private enterprise and loyalty to one's government are irresistibly opposed. Milo himself remains innocently unaware of this adversarial relationship since one of his unquestioned assumptions is that the whole reason for government is to promote such capitalistic undertakings as M & M Enterprises. Such thinking explains how he can consistently act against the government and yet maintain his conviction that his acts serve the country's best interests. For his acts are always within the bounds of the law, and he actually perceives legal loopholes as benign sanctions to encourage creative business ventures. Heller refers to his "rigid scruples that would not even allow him to borrow a package of pitted dates . . . for the food at the mess hall was all still the property of the government." But he nonetheless feels completely at liberty to borrow a package from Yossarian in order to make a profit for himself—or rather for the syndicate, whose continuing growth is the sole criterion dreamt of in his philosophy.

It is obvious that his "rigid scruples" compel him to obey strictly the letter of the law but permit him utterly to disregard the law's spirit. Thus his informing Yossarian, "with a faint glimmer of mischief," that he has "a sure-fire plan for cheating the federal government out of six thousand dollars" does not contradict his expressed obedience to the law, since his venture, we may assume, is not illegal but ingeniously exploitative of legality. He is able to confide in Yossarian because, as Heller very suggestively has had him reflect earlier, "anyone who would not steal from the country he loved would not steal from anybody." By the same token, however, Yossarian's genuine respect for his nation's ideals guarantees his instant dismissal of Milo's offer to make him a partner in his machinations. Milo's legally shrewd (but morally obtuse) mind is also blatantly evident in his rationalizing to the detached Yossarian—throughout the novel Milo's foil and the moral yardstick that enables us to measure his essential dishonesty—that although "bribery is against the law . . . it's not against the law to make a profit. . . . So it can't be against the law for me to bribe someone in order to make a fair [read "whatever-the-market-will-bear"] profit. . . ."

Because, psychologically, Milo's dominant need is to control reality, to bend it to his unruly ego, it follows that he will be opposed to anything that threatens to limit that control. Governmental restraints have always been set on free enterprise, so that Milo, at the same time that he perceives his financial opportunism as licensed by his country's capitalistic ethic, cannot but acknowledge the power of government to restrict his commercial ventures, or to prohibit them altogether. Consequently, his enlarging the scope of his operations to include not only the trading of foodstuffs but the bombing of enemy targets—the enemy determined simply by the country contracting for the bombing—indicates that for Milo the war is actually against government itself. For to Milo the ultimate cause is not freedom but free enterprise, and the battle will be finally won only when war too is controlled not by government but by industrious individuals like himself. When war becomes but one more business to be manipulated by the enterprising, Milo's control of reality—or rather his fantasy of such control—will be complete. As crazy, or morally insane, as this characterization of Milo's unarticulated delusions may seem, it is a reading that derives naturally from Milo's expressed sentiments. After contracting with both American and German authorities to attack—and defend—the German-held bridge at Orvieto, the self-congratulatory Milo explains that "the consummation of these deals represented an important victory for private enterprise . . . since the armies of both countries were socialized institutions."

While such thinking suggests not only Milo's moral myopia but his derangement as well, in the mentally and morally unbalanced world of the novel it escapes condemnation. We learn, for instance, that when Milo raids his own squadron for the Germans the public uproar is stilled once he discloses the enormous profits earned in the deal for the syndicate and convinces everyone "that bombing his own men and plans had therefore really been a commendable and very lucrative blow on the side of private enterprise." Since, as Heller sees it, virtually everyone today needs desperately to believe that he has not been left out—that it is no myth that he owns a share, has a piece of the action, and profits as GM profits—Milo's heinous crimes (and he is quite literally an enemy of the people) are easily enough rationalized as heroic. Here again an action—and reaction—that is realistically incredible or absurd can be seen as a figuratively—and frighteningly—accurate picture of a people profoundly alienated from a government grown so vast and impersonal as to make them feel powerless. As morally insane as Milo obviously is, his sentiments express those of millions of his countrymen, who rebelliously, yet somehow innocently, crave membership in an organization so large and potent as to be beyond the control of the law. Such "quiet desperation" is betrayed by the public's appallingly uncritical lionization of Milo and his ruthless exploits. And the painful irony and ultimate self-victimization of such moral viciousness is poignantly suggested by the author himself, who has commented:

> . . . the content of the book really derives from our present atmosphere, which is one of chaos, of disorganization, of absurdity, of cruelty, of brutality, of insensitivity, but at the same time one in which people, even the worst people, I think are basically good, are motivated by humane impulses.

Since Milo's perverted idealism makes him deplore governmental regulation of business and its virtual "monopolization" of war, it is no surprise that after attacking his own base he decides not to reimburse his country for its losses. His hypocritical argument is that since "in a democracy, the government is the people . . . we might just as well keep the money and eliminate the middleman." Then, shifting his rhetorical ground so suddenly that his glaring self-contradictions may be conveniently overlooked by everyone, he adds:

> Frankly, I'd like to see the government get out of war altogether and leave the whole field to private industry. If we pay the government everything we owe it, we'll only be encouraging government control and discouraging other individuals from bombing their own men and planes. We'll be taking away their incentive.

This absurd laissez-faire attitude is responsible for Milo's "hawkish" stance on war, which derives not from any political ideals but from purely economic concerns. War *is* profitable to private industry, and Milo has no desire to see it end. When it suits his purpose, he may profess that he is "willing to do everything [he can] to win the war," but the pretense and self-deception of his words is demonstrated by his negotiations calculated expressly to prolong the combat as long as strategically possible. Heller writes, for example, of his "selling petroleum and ball bearings to Germany at good prices in order to make a good profit and help maintain a balance of power between the contending forces."

Milo's childishly naïve conception of his world as something to be manipulated for the best possible gain is of course at the heart of his moral insanity. And Heller allows the reader no doubt that the radically self-centered ethic which makes Milo so contemptible is representative—however hyperbolically—of our culture. Surely it is no coincidence that the author has General Peckem state: "People have a right to do anything that's not forbidden by law" and Doc Daneeka defensively proclaim: "There's nothing wrong with greed." That through the course of American history the ideal of freedom should have become so corrupted as to be popularly construed to mean the right to do anything and everything not strictly prohibited by law is perhaps the deepest tragedy of the book. Yossarian's harsh indictment of the monstrously "principled" opportunism that has too often been the consequence of a capitalistic ethic is eloquently expressed at the novel's conclusion when he observes: "When I look up, I see people cashing in. I don't see heavens or saints or angels. I see people cashing in on every decent impulse and every human tragedy." Milo, mercilessly "cashing in" on the war itself, is the all-too-human predator of good will and bad fortune who best exemplifies Yossarian's profoundly discouraged estimate. It is Milo who tries to persuade him to swallow non-edible cotton, as it is Milo who robs his planes of the carbon dioxide for the life jackets, and their marketable parachutes and medical supplies. And in every instance Milo's treachery has been innocently motivated by the one principle in which all his mistaken faith resides: namely, "what's good for M & M Enterprises. . . ." The essential falseness of this principle is evident from the falseness of the syndicate's title, since the "&" in "M & M" has been inserted by Milo to avoid the impression that the operation is that of a single individual. But conjunction or not, the abbreviation still spells out to "Milo and Minderbinder" and points, however deviously, to individual ownership and control.

Since Milo's acts are so corrupt, it is only natural to infer that given his popularity and power he is responsible for corrupting others. In fact, the name "Minderbinder" may be possibly have been contrived to suggest Milo's amazing "binding of minds" through his steady deluge of self-serving capitalistic rhetoric. It is safest to conclude, however, that Milo does little more than supply the rationalization for his followers' own selfish endeavors to fulfill purely personal ends, and that both Milo and his admirers are best understood as products of a system which has itself corrupted them. For it is the system that has somehow fostered their belief that as free citizens their birthright, indeed their very duty, is competitively to pursue individual interests at every opportunity. Milo merely succeeds in tempting those he deals with to follow inclinations inherited from their culture anyway. Very early in his enterprises, he is able to talk Major —— de Coverly into furnishing him with a plane and pilot to purchase eggs from Malta and butter from Sicily because the Major himself admits to a weakness for fresh eggs and butter. Given the infantile self-indulgence of so many of Heller's characters, the sequel to this action is only to be expected:

> Then the other three squadrons in Colonel Cathcart's group turned their mess halls over to Milo and gave him an airplane and a pilot each so that he could buy fresh eggs and fresh butter for them too. Milo's planes shuttled back and forth seven days a week as every officer in the four squadrons began devouring fresh eggs in an insatiable orgy of fresh-egg eating.

So that this highly specialized egg orgy should not exhaust itself and thereby reduce his influence over the officers, Milo locates plentiful sources for "fresh veal, beef, duck, baby lamb chops, mushroom caps, broccoli, South African rock lobster tails, shrimp, hams, puddings, grapes, ice cream, strawberries and artichokes." His remarkable success in appealing to the officers' oral drives in fact points to their generally infantile stage of development—moral as well as psychological—and hints at their almost total lack of fellow feeling. The widespread passion for eating and obtaining food in the novel seems to have displaced the traditional desire for love and family. At one isolated point we learn that Milo is actually married and has a family, but it is clear that Milo's mind and heart exist elsewhere. The author remarks that "in the spring Milo Minderbinder's fancy . . . lightly turned to thoughts of tangerines," and Milo himself glibly translates the language of parental love to livestock when he describes his black market lamb chops as dressed "in the cutest little pink paper panties you ever saw."

The ultimate hazards posed by Milo's simple-minded transference of interest from people to profit are alluded to by Heller, who has commented of Milo's psychodynamics: "I gave him a mental and moral simplicity that, to my mind, makes him a horrifyingly dangerous person, because he lacks evil intent." Milo's "mental and moral simplicity" enables him to find easy justifications for everything he is impelled to do, so that while his acts may frequently appear hypocritical or deceitful, they are nonetheless executed sincerely and with moral courage. However morally insane his conduct may seem—and however satirically Heller may present it—it always reflects the "purity" of his deeply felt principles:

> With a devotion to purpose above and beyond the line of duty, he . . . raised the price of food in his mess halls so high that all the officers and enlisted men had to turn over all their pay to him in order to eat. Their alternative—there was an alternative, of course, since Milo detested coercion and was a vocal champion of freedom of choice—was to starve. When he encountered a wave of enemy resistance to this attack, he stuck to his position without regard for his safety or reputation and gallantly invoked the law of supply and demand. And when someone somewhere said no, Milo gave ground grudgingly, valiantly defending, even in retreat, the historic right of free men to pay as much as they had to for the things they needed in order to survive.

Such morally perverted reasoning occurs throughout the novel, and it should be recognized that Heller does not at all limit it to Milo. Doc Daneeka lies outrageously to the government in a desperate bid to escape military service, and when inevitably he is found out can only lament that "even the word of a licensed physician is suspected by the country he loves." Chief White Halfoat inveighs against racial prejudice and then adds self-righteously that "it's a terrible thing to treat a decent, loyal Indian like a nigger, kike, wop or spic." And Colonel Cathcart, after making a wholly unscrupulous deal with the glory-hungry Milo to credit him with missions that the other men must fly for him, responds to the mess officer's request that his friend Yossarian be spared from such missions with genuine shock: "Oh, no Milo. . . .We must never play favorites. We must always treat every man alike."

The absurd self-deceptiveness and even the flagrant hypocrisy manifest in these and numerous other incidents, point, though with consummate irony, to the basically "good heart" of Heller's morally mad characters. Moreover, as incredibly callous as Doc Daneeka is portrayed, when his base is bombed (compliments of M & M Enterprises), he freely places his life in peril and works himself to exhaustion striving to save as many lives as possible. As criminally insensitive as Colonel Cathcart is, when General Dreedle is on the verge of having Major Danby shot for an imagined offense, Cathcart yearns to comfort the terrified Major—though he refrains from doing so because he fears looking "like a sissy." Milo's good will is evident in several places, though his finally brutal economic commitments regularly subvert his benign intentions. When Yossarian implores his assistance in locating Nately's whore's defenseless kid sister in Rome, he readily agrees to help and is so moved by the nobility of Yossarian's disinterested search as to exclaim: ". . . we'll find that girl if we have to turn this whole city upside down." Later Milo abandons Yossarian at police headquarters when he accidentally learns of the huge profits to be made in smuggling tobacco; but the author makes it difficult to condemn him, emphasizing that the prospect of such a lucrative venture actually leaves Milo defenseless himself, "as though he were in the grip of a blind fixation, burning feverishly, and his twitching mouth slavering." The passion or "lust" described here is, of course, greed, but since Milo is pictured more as its helpless victim that as its god, and since he is not without attractive personal traits, it is hard to withhold all sympathy from him. Heller himself has spoken of Milo as acting "out of the goodness of his heart" and admitted: "Yossarian is actually fond of Milo, and I am too, as an individual. There's a certain purity of purpose about him."

Still Heller is careful to identify Milo as the one character in the book who "does the most damage." For while Milo's motives may be untainted and his heart undefiled, his conscience—thoroughly pledged to the profit principle dominant in our age—is totally corrupt, compelling him to commit acts cruel and harmful to humanity. Such is the nature of Milo's absurd innocence: a finally pathetic moral deformity that must be judged culpable because of the serious threats it poses to the peace, freedom, happiness, and even the lives of others. Generally the most understanding critical assessment of Milo is one by Wayne Charles Miller:

> Milo is not an insidious and conniving power-hungry fascist. In fact, it is testament to Heller's genius that he could create a figure simultaneously so innocent and so destructive as is his representative of American business values and perhaps capitalism itself. Milo is frightening precisely because he is such a perfect product of the culture. Industrious, competent, pleasant, engaging, sexually moral or perhaps sexless, he is destined for success. In fact, Milo is the kind of son that most American parents wish their boys to be. . . .

If, then, Milo is not simply a bad seed, it is clearly his culture that has warped his moral growth. The author writes of his "disunited eyes," which "could see more things than most people, but . . . could see none of them too distinctly"; and this obviously symbolic description intimates that Milo's vision is hopelessly defective, that he is unable to distinguish between serving his country and exploiting it. A similar situation obtains with the syndicate: he idealistically envisions it as affirming humanity (since "everyone has a share") at the same time that his bedazzled commitment to it leads him systematically to trample on the rights of others. The only standard by which he is equipped to appraise action is monetary, so that his preternaturally shrewd business sense is matched by a moral sense so obtuse, so astoundingly irrational and unaware, that finally we can see it only as insane. Because Milo literally lacks the perspective to see his world whole, or to decipher the moral dimensions of his conduct, blaming him for his perverse adherence to short-sighted, morally reprehensible principles may be a little like blaming a deaf man for not listening to what is said to him. Milo's principles do not *prohibit* fellow feeling or empathy, nor is Heller's testifying to his "good heart" a gratuitous assertion. Yet Milo's emotional priorities are such that his genuine compassion for humanity is always overwhelmed by his humanly monstrous passion for money. For example, when he is informed by Yossarian that the funeral he is witnessing is Snowden's, this is his reaction:

> "That's terrible," Milo grieved, and his large brown eyes filled with tears. "That poor kid. It really is terrible." He bit his trembling lip hard, and his voice rose with emotion when he continued. "And it will get even worse if the mess halls don't agree to buy my cotton."

This crucial deficiency of feeling is evidenced throughout the novel, and it is most exasperating as it reveals Milo's almost complete absence of moral responsibility, which allows him to contract with the enemy for the deaths of his own men without experiencing the slightest pangs of conscience. For, as he rationalizes to Yossarian, what he undertook for the Germans would have been undertaken anyway; and besides, his business deals with them are very profitable for the syndicate, of which Yossarian himself owns a share. Milo's enduring belief that he is innocent of the deaths for which he has, however unwittingly, made himself morally responsible, underlies his self-righteous protests that he did not start the war, that he is "just trying to put it on a businesslike basis." His absolute denial of any complicity with evil comes in his ensuing question: "Is anything wrong with that?", and suggests a conviction of guiltlessness, or even moral superiority, that perhaps only the most guilty may be capable of feeling.

If Milo's finally culpable innocence stems from his relating to all things as commodities, so does his rampant opportunism—and in the end these two predilections are practically indistinguishable. Together they account for Milo's extraordinary accomplishments as a businessman. Because the author pessimistically views the world as one "in which success was the only virtue," it is no wonder that Milo, the great entrepreneur, becomes something of a world idol in the novel. Stimulating business around the globe, a veritable high priest of commerce, he becomes almost everybody's hero and is showered with adoration and political titles. In one especially parodic chapter, "Milo the Mayor," we learn that in recognition of his having brought the Scotch trade to Sicily he has been elected Mayor of Palermo, Carini, Monreale, Bagheria, Termini Imerese, Cefalu, Mistretta, and Nicosia; that for bringing the egg trade to Malta he has been named its Assistant Governor-General; that he is Vice-Shah of Oran, Caliph of Baghdad, Imam of Damascus, and Sheik of Araby; and that in parts of Africa he is the reigning corn god, rain god, and rice god. In America, Milo fares equally well, being a paragon of corporate know-how and success. The thinly veiled acerbity of Heller's satire against the almost universal acceptance of free enterprise and the inhumane values so carelessly authorized by it is conspicuous in the lines: "Milo had been caught red-handed in the act of plundering his countrymen, and, as a result, his stock had never been higher." The admiration and respect accorded him betrays the American worship of material success over all else and its need to identify with individual accomplishment by assiduously cultivating the illusion—created initially by the business tycoons themselves—that "everyone has a share" and that "what's good for M & M Enterprises is good for the country." Heller finds various ways of generalizing this heedless pursuit of material well-being, just one of them being Nurse Duckett's casual abandonment of Yossarian because she "had decided to marry a doctor—any doctor, because they all did so well in business. . . ."

Exemplifying in caricature form the monetary drives of most of the populace, Milo is driven by the same socially divisive but culturally endorsed quest for wealth and power. He is therefore not identifiable in the novelistic context either as amoral or immoral. For his morality, rooted firmly in the laws of modern economics, does not really run counter to that of his culture. The crucial point is that Milo is moral according to the absurd, morally insane, standards which prevail; but viewed from any traditional set of ethical norms he is corrupt—exactly as corrupt as the culture whose unofficial but universally practiced ethic he embodies and whose madly utilitarian vindication of his lucrative but literally murderous bombing of his own base carries its own condemnation. If Milo's country allows such outrageous misbehavior to go unpunished (and Heller has admitted that its doing so can only be understood allegorically), it is because Milo's acts are in essential conformity with his country's institutional framework. Its gross insensitivity to the lives of its average citizens is an outcome of its wildly discriminatory power structure.

Again, the evil that Milo and others depict is not the result of something peculiarly sinister about them but the outcome of their lacking what in the novel is referred to as "character," a deficit that allows them to take advantage of their bureaucratic positions to pursue worldly success as their culture implicitly advocates. If they pervert the original meaning of freedom, it is because the capitalistic system to which they owe their greatest allegiance has in its evolution already perverted it. All they have done has been to react with "moral and mental simplicity" (i.e., innocently) to its apparent message and, in a most "democratic" spirit, compete relentlessly to achieve more than their fellow man.

Such opportunism stems from a curiously willful innocence and grows into the full-fledged moral insanity that best defines the absurdity everywhere present in *Catch-22*. It is a world in which even the dull Major Major eventually learns that, practically, sinning and lying are good for him. Such an insight does not really come as a surprise, we are told, "for he had observed that people who did lie were, on the whole, more resourceful and ambitious and successful than people who did not lie." Much later in the novel the singularly virtuous chaplain must admit, after he has told his first lie, that the results are "wonderful." Deliberately parodying Genesis in language identical to that used to describe Major Major's unholy discovery, Heller writes, "The chaplain had sinned, and it was good," adding in a now famous passage:

> . . . everyone knew that sin was evil and that no good could come from evil. But he did feel good; he felt positively marvelous. Consequently, it followed logically that telling lies and defecting from duty could not be sins. The chaplain had mastered, in a moment of divine intuition, the handy technique of protective rationalization. . . . It was almost no trick at all, he saw, to turn vice into virtue and slander into truth, impotence into abstinence, arrogance into humility, plunder into philanthropy, thievery into honor, blasphemy into wisdom, brutality into patriotism, and sadism into justice. Anybody could do it; it required no brains at all. It merely required no character.

While the chaplain has enough character to resist giving way to his demonic conclusions, events quickly make him realize just how widely the military bureaucracy has been seduced—or rather, corrupted—by them. In one of the novel's most terrifying scenes, he is taken to a cellar and brutally questioned by a group of officers about violations he has not committed. His interrogators "handily" find him guilty of everything they charge him with, including "crimes and infractions" which, they readily confess, they "don't even know about yet." After this travesty of justice is completed, the chaplain's alarm is replaced by "overwhelming moral outrage"; and more daring than ever before, he confronts Colonel Korn with his righteous protests—only, once again, to be confounded by the "immoral logic" of the colonel's unfeeling response.

This "immoral logic" is clearly the logic of opportunism, and it consists of all the "protective rationalizations" that hopelessly pervert all meaningful moral standards. The moral insanity that results from such reasoning is abundantly evident throughout the book, and it is perhaps most blatant in Korn's incongruous reasoning with Yossarian at the end of the novel, when he and Cathcart craftily attempt to remove the threat to their authority created by the bombardier's insubordination by returning him home a hero. Korn offhandedly discloses to Yossarian that his not really deserving to be exempted from further combat is one of the reasons he does not mind exempting him. Similarly insane is Cathcart's rationalization for raising the men's missions: the pilot McWatt's accidental mutilation of Kid Sampson and McWatt's own consequent suicide. And so, of course, is his raising them again once he learns from an official flight form that a Doc Daneeka has been on board the fated plane. The fact that Doc Daneeka has not actually been on the flight does not affect the colonel's decision, for the written document is all his debased moral sense requires to justify his determination to make his men fly more missions than anyone else, in the hope of attaining the professional advancement he craves. His thinking, however moral he may self-deceptively consider it, is purely opportunistic and closely resembles that of the power-seeking Captain Black, whose "Glorious Loyalty Oath Crusade" is motivated not by any genuine patriotic feeling (despite what the Captain himself might think) but by the desire to become "a man of real consequence" in the squadron and maybe even replace Major Major (who is not permitted to sign the oaths) as squadron commander.

The crowning symbol of all this uncontrolled opportunism is "Catch-22," which is most meaningfully defined by the forsaken old woman in Rome, who tells Yossarian (echoing the old "might makes right" idea) that "Catch-22 says they [here specifically the MP's but in essence most people everywhere] have a right to do anything we can't stop them from doing." In this late scene we learn that Catch-22 is not merely the label for all the morally crazy double binds in the novel but the summary explanation of these binds: namely, that to achieve recognition, assert power, or attain wealth most people can, and will, do almost anything they think they can get away with doing. Given any social, political, or economic system designed primarily to safeguard individualism and only secondarily to safeguard individuals, moral chaos must be the result. The horrible irony of this situation is that this humanly unaccountable law of opportunism was never intended as a law at all, was never meant by those who founded government, particularly *our* government, to become a national creed. Yossarian reveals an awareness of this tragic misinterpretation of the nation's original purpose in his pained reflection that "Catch-22 did not exist . . . but it made no difference. What did matter was that everyone thought it existed, and that was much worse. . . ." Yossarian has a glimpse of the awful truth which is Catch-22: not only that a corrupt American officialdom has been confused with America but that the entire nation is helplessly victimized by accepting as official, written law all the unscrupulous power ploys that seem sanctioned by a democratic government. Or, to put it somewhat differently, unwritten loopholes in the laws have become confused with the laws themselves, enabling those in positions of authority to trespass freely on the rights of others. In addition, "freedom from" has been misconstrued as "freedom to," so that almost everyone regards himself as "bound" to be in opposition to everyone else in pursuing life, liberty, and happiness.

Such a circumstance accounts for the fact that the real enemy in the novel is not the other side but our own. General Peckem's remarks that "Dreedle's on our side, and Dreedle *is* the enemy" and that "General Dreedle commands four bomb groups that we simply must capture in order to continue our offensive" sharply expose the destructive competitiveness that identifies us as a country fundamentally at war with ourselves. Quite literally in the novel, we are our own worst enemy. Milo's freely appropriating the morphine from the squadron's planes to market it as he deems fit provides further symbolic testimony of how individualism, degraded in practice to mere opportunism, can only increase our suffering.

It should be stressed that the object of Heller's attack is not America per se but those people whose greedy exploitation of it compromises the peace and freedom of others—though, to be sure, this distinction is at times extremely difficult to maintain. For those who control our various systems and institutions ultimately make our country what it is. Still both Heller and Yossarian insist on the distinction; and it is right that they do so. When Colonel Korn asks Yossarian, "Won't you fight for your country? . . . Won't you give up your life for Colonel Cathcart and me?" Yossarian shows his final comprehension of all that has transpired by retorting, "What have you and Colonel Cathcart got to do with my country? You're not the same." However indirectly, this climactic scene has been anticipated almost from the very beginning when the author, speaking in his own voice, notes: "All over the world, boys on every side of the bomb line were laying down their lives for *what they had been told* [emphasis added] was their country. . . ."

Catch-22 itself is not intended to symbolize America but what those in command have reduced it to. And it is the moral wickedness which Catch-22 stands for that constitutes the greatest threat to Yossarian's existence. Most significantly, it is Catch-22 that forces him to go on flying missions after he should have been recognized as fulfilling his obligations. At one point, Doc Daneeka tells Yossarian that "Catch-22 . . . says you've always got to do what your commanding officer tells you to." And when Yossarian protests that Twenty-Seventh Air Force Headquarters states that he can go home after forty missions (he now has forty-eight), Doc Daneeka counters irresistibly: "But they don't say you have to go home. And regulations do say you have to obey every order. That's the catch." At another point, Yossarian gets Doc Daneeka to concede that if he fills out a medical form testifying to his unfitness he can have him removed from combat status. But once again Catch-22 renders this action worthless since Group must approve the form and, as Doc Daneeka very well knows, "Group isn't going to." Yossarian is effectively stripped of all his rights not so much by the law as by a bureaucratic system that is at base totalitarian. In this system all men are not created equal, so that Yossarian is in fact a captive held by his own side. That the higher authority to which he must submit is as immoral as it is irrational is shown by the fact that he is kept on active combat status even when replacements for him are readily available and the Allies are virtually assured of victory.

The deviousness of the peremptory nonlaw which is Catch-22 is best suggested by the "innocently" authoritative Milo. For Milo's specifically economic ideals are at bottom almost synonymous with the ideals of all the other systems attacked in the novel. His charging whatever the traffic will bear for his goods and services (in the name of free enterprise) is hardly different, for example, from Cathcart's endlessly raising the number of missions his men must fly (in the name of patriotism). The true motive in each case is opportunism, or on a more basic level, the need or compulsion to assert one's will over others. And the sanction for such tyrannical assertion is Catch-22, since in essence it *means* the right to do whatever one can manage to do with impunity. When Milo tells Yossarian that "he was jeopardizing his traditional rights of freedom and independence by daring to exercise them," the context suggests that Milo's hypocritical warning is inspired by his subliminal awareness that should Yossarian continue to revolt by, ironically, affirming his rights—and prompt others to follow him—the system itself, of which Milo is metaphorically the leader, would crumble. To survive, the system depends on the cooperation of the oppressed with the oppressors, and once the oppressed remonstrate against the Catch-22 framework which dehumanizes them, the system—supported by the most tenuous legal foundations in any case—cannot but disintegrate. But Heller, a most sober realist, really has no such expectations that *Catch-22*'s supremacy will ever be effectively challenged, for so long as the masses never recognize its existence as a fabrication of ambitious individuals to achieve and preserve personal power, they must remain impotent to resist its dubious authority.

Dr. Stubbs, one of the novel's most positively handled characters, says of Yossarian: "That crazy bastard may be the only sane one left," and his paradoxical appraisal helps point out Yossarian's difficulties. Because Yossarian refuses to submit, robotlike, to the system and persists in his efforts to defy it, he is perceivable as insane, incapable of adapting to the social and moral norms of his time. But because he alone seems capable of appreciating the sanctity of life and its desecration by all the spiritually void authorities who would gratuitously rob him of it, he is ultimately to be perceived as the novel's "hero" of sanity. He has, however, little in common with the traditional hero, since while he may offer minor frustrations to the enemy (the villain-system of opportunism) he cannot begin to alter its morally insane structure. His only alternative, then, is not to fight but to flee, and the novel's romantic-realistic conclusion attests to Yossarian's unvanquishable humanity—as well as to the tragic untenability of this humanity. But although his impassioned effort to leave all the Milo's of the modern world behind him and locate an area where sane moral commitments prevail may indeed be futile, there is no denying its integrity and courage. And here, for one last time, it is fitting to bring in the comments of the author:

> Now, in Yossarian's situation—his environment, his society, the world; and it's not just America, it's the world itself—the monolithic society closes off every conventional area of protest or corrective action, and the only choice that's left to him is one of ignoble acceptance in which he can profit and live very comfortably—but nevertheless ignoble—or *flight*, a renunciation of that condition, of that society, that set of circumstances.
>
> The only way he can renounce it without going to jail is by deserting it, trying to keep going until they capture him. I like to think of him as a kind of spirit on the loose. You know, he is the only hope left at the end of the book. Had he accepted that choice. . . .

MARCUS K. BILLSON III

The Un-Minderbinding of Yossarian: Genesis Inverted in Catch-22

The temptation of Yossarian in Joseph Heller's *Catch-22* alludes to one of our oldest texts in the West, our Judeo-Christian myth of origins. At Snowden's funeral, Yossarian identifies with Adam as he sits naked in the tree of the knowledge of good and evil. Like his prototype in the garden of Eden, Yossarian is reduced to gaping mutely at the mystery of death. Like Adam, he was "born in . . . innocence" and generally prefers nudity to the wearing of clothes. Similar to his ancient forebear, he is Semitic. Yet, unlike his predecessor, Yossarian rejects his tempter, Milo Minderbinder, and thus does not reenact the crucial failure. This important reversal of the original scenario significantly dismantles the old myth in the novel.

Heller's allusion to Genesis suggests the lineaments of an intertexuality between the Bible and the novel, which exists within and without literary history: within, since the novel derives meaning and irony from its reference to Genesis; without, because the novel undermines the first text's historical status as it promotes a new parable of origins, and because the novel challenges the earlier text's historical authority by revealing that a former text can be fruitfully understood by means of a latter. In discussing the two texts together, I shall be exploring a particular attitude about the operation of language and observing how this attitude affects the myth of beginnings of our Judeo-

From *The Arizona Quarterly* 36, no. 4. © 1980 by the Arizona Board of Regents.

Christian culture and in turn discloses what has remained heretofore concealed in the novel.

On the second page of *Catch-22*, Yossarian observes the ability of language to create and destroy whole worlds of experience, as he sits censoring letters in his hospital bed. From then on, the novel tells a tale of Yossarian's growing awareness of the destructive functions of language. As the written word, language obliterates such characters as Mudd and Luciana. Lt. Mudd never signed up in the squadron, so that when he is killed in action over Orvieto he cannot be reported dead. Since language does not certify his death, it will not certify his life, and Lt. Mudd is ruthlessly dropped by the Air Corps bureaucracy as if he had never existed at all. Yossarian eliminates Luciana's existence when he tears up her address in a fit of machismo. Try as he does to find her afterwards in all the places she is supposed to be, he is unsuccessful; the written word destroyed is reality annihilated. As the interrogations of Clevinger and the chaplain prove, spoken language can also be easily used as a machine-weapon to indict man into an inexorable, gratuitous guilt. Moreover, language insidiously confounds through the very ambiguity of its meaning, perpetrating disorder and chaos. Patriotism in the novel, for example, means both loyalty and active devotion to the country as well as the perversion and excess of that loyalty in the name of which every form of brutality can be committed. For Heller, patriotism comes to mean not only allegiance to American democracy, but also the institutionalized tyranny and exploitation of the military system supposedly carried on in the country's best interests. Patriotism, like sanity in the world of *Catch-22*, is confusing, possessing a positive connotation which ironically generates its opposite. The opposite connotation then calls attention to the positive meaning even while it displaces it. Hence, the concept of patriotism possesses no concrete, absolute value, and Heller's novel delights in showing the absurdity implicit in thinking that it does.

The destructive power of language codified into rules, regulations, and systems is, of course, epitomized by the catch-all catch-can Catch-22. As Doc Daneeka first explains it, Catch-22 is that military rule used to explain why both sane and insane must continue to fly their missions:

> There was one catch and that was Catch-22, which specified that a concern for one's own safety in the face of dangers that were real and immediate was the process of a rational mind. Orr was crazy and could be grounded. All he had to do was ask; and as soon as he did, he would no longer be crazy and would have to fly more missions. Orr would be crazy to fly more missions and sane if he didn't, but if he was sane he had to fly them. If he flew

them he was crazy and didn't have to; but if he didn't want to he was sane and had to.

There is no way out of the tautological absurdity of a regulation that asserts only the sane have to fly, to kill, and to die, and that men are only too sane when they don't want to do these things and ask to be relieved from them. The second definition of Catch-22 reinforces the circular logic of all totalitarianism based on an a priori authority that is not actually present: "Catch-22 . . . says you've always got to do what your commanding officer tells you to." The final definition of Catch-22 accounts for all the others and is explained to Yossarian by the old woman in the raided whorehouse in Rome: "Catch-22 says they have a right to do anything we can't stop them from doing." The "they" can refer to the MPs who have driven the whores out onto the streets, but the pronoun also refers to any authority supported by the system of language. The will of authority predominates by the force of language. Man is caught in an unrelenting cycle of oppression and brutality disguised in the convolutions of Catch-22. Born into behavioral patterns and social institutions which are first structured and then transmogrified by language, man has difficulty coping with this authority which seems immanent, yet is never really present in language. It is against this cycle that Yossarian rebels: "Someone had to do something sometime. Every victim was a culprit, every culprit a victim, and somebody had to stand up sometime to try and break the lousy chain of inherited habit that was imperiling them all."

Yossarian comes to find that the sinister Schopenhaueresque expression of will is the "inherited habit" of language. Man has witlessly locked himself into a brutal and absurd form of behavior, predicated upon a mindless obedience to all those authorities never really present in Catch-22. Catch-22 is law deriving its power from a universal act of faith in language as presence. That is, a faith that language and the thing, thus language and the world, are one. For those in the novel, this means that language finally becomes the prime experience—not just the record of experience. The world of the novel projects the horrific, yet all too real, power of language to divest itself from any necessity of reference, to function as an independent, totally autonomous medium with its own perfect system and logic. That such a language pretends to mirror anything but itself is a commonplace delusion which Heller satirizes masterfully throughout the novel. Yet, civilization is informed by this very pretense, and Heller shows how man is tragically and comically tricked and manipulated by such an absurdity.

As an example, Heller playfully inverts the concepts of sanity and insanity, revealing the absurdity of their referring to anything other than a merely provisional linguistic coherence. Heller frustrates reader anticipation as he demonstrates that sane and insane refer not to rational or irrational behavior outside language, but only pretend to such reference, while in actuality deferring all cogent, consistent reference entirely. The legalisms of Catch-22 may define an action or person as sane or insane, but such definitions turn in upon themselves and are binding only for the moment. In seeking to preserve his life, Yossarian acts in what he considers to be a sane manner, but in the verbal consensus of the novel, his actions are often considered to be insane, because they consistently work for his survival and thereby negate the destructive expediences of Catch-22 maintained by the prevailing powers. Sanity, for the world of the novel, is meaningless as a cogent definition and evaluation of behavior, since it is simply the condition of believing in whatever the prevailing authority claims to be sane at the time.

In a subtle but brilliant sally, Heller returns to the first literate myth of origins in Judeo-Christian culture, the Book of Genesis, to undo the very story of beginnings which initiated the treadmill habit of believing in language as presence and which began the enslavement of man by language. Before examining Heller's scene in the novel, let us consider the second and third chapters of Genesis (especially the temptation and fall) in light of the ineluctable tyranny implicit in the meaning of Catch-22. The novel becomes the source of a key concept necessary for an understanding of an earlier text, as we find that Genesis 2-3 posits the first Catch-22. In the Garden of Eden, a law was promulgated which offered an analogously absurd logic for human suffering and evil. God's third speech to man is an enunciation of a law. Genesis 2:16-17 reads: "You may freely eat of every tree of the garden; but of the tree of the knowledge of good and evil you shall not eat, for in the day that you eat of it you shall die." This first law holds an especially subtle sway over the consciousness of man. Adam does not yet know the meaning of death. Yet, this law commands him to accept names without available meaning, categories without substance; it proposes an order based on faith rather than reason. God's words to man reveal language's role as a vehicle for the law, and, simultaneously, they reveal law itself as a rigidification of the order language imposes on experience. The first law appears to grant man freedom to do what he wants, to eat of *every* tree, but this permission is immediately curtailed by a negative injunction. In bliss or in pain, this law will abide; it is incontrovertible, unremitting, and eternal because Adam accepts it. In the *Weltanschauung* of Genesis, he has no other choice. Man's fall is predetermined and inscribed in the very use of language to enunciate the law. Employing the language of man to communicate to Adam, God expropriates language for the expression of His will. At the very moment of God's first speech to Adam, the authors of Genesis necessitate Adam's fall, because only in failing the law can man understand God's absolute authority and power, and only through the fall can the meaning of the law itself become intelligible.

Hence, whatever man did in the garden of Eden, he was the loser. If he remained in innocence, he would live without knowledge; if he chose knowledge, he would live in pain. God's will is imposed either way, and like the universe of Catch-22, there is no way for man to beat the system either through obedience or disobedience as long as he continues to believe that the law originates in an immanent higher authority. That man can only know good through evil (i.e., difference) is one of the consolations of the *felix culpa*, but the mechanism of this paradox is, nevertheless, a Catch-22. Man cannot know good until he has sinned, and the wages of sin are pain, toil, and death. In Eden, the law has no meaning unless disobeyed. Like children, Adam and Eve know nothing of their parent's power, fiercefulness, and retribution until they have suffered the consequences of their transgression. In Genesis, suffering for knowledge becomes the fate of man. Yet, this suffering determines man's status as a loser. From birth he inherits the necessity to sin and the imperative of guilt as long as he desires to know, as long as knowledge and meaning are objects of human effort.

When Adam and Eve believe that knowledge and the fruit of the tree are one, they are innocent of meaning, and the power of the law is sustained through faith. But Adam and Eve come to realize that the knowledge of good and evil is not the fruit of the tree. Knowledge results from the act of disobedience against a privileged law. Thus, knowledge is violence to the word of God, violence to the faith of the word as presence. In Genesis, this violence must entail retributive suffering, if the power and authority of God are to be credible. However, meaning is always violence to the word as presence. The word cannot mean without an awareness of the absence in the word of that to which it refers. God may have named death to Adam, but He does not really inform man of the meaning of death and the consequences of sin before the transgression. The fall of Adam is man's fall into an awareness of meaning, an awareness of the difference between the word and the thing.

Before the fall, Adam was unable to make a fully informed choice, incapable of understanding what God had said and what He had meant. Therefore, man's free will is born with Adam's learning the significance of meaning rather than merely naming. The myth of the fall can be seen, therefore, as man's discovery of meaning in its fullest, most problematic sense, not just as signification, but as ambiguity as well. Within the limits of language, the fall was necessary for man to learn the operation of meaning. Through the fall, Adam and Eve come to comprehend that the signified "death" is but a metaphor for another signifier, "sin," that in turn is a metaphor for disobedience, which is a metaphor for violence to the law of God, which is a metaphor for knowledge, and so on. Hence, meaning is generated in man's knowledge not of the presence, but of the difference of language, and in Adam's perception of language as a metaphorical operation itself: his awareness that the word functions as the dynamic tension between the possibility of likeness (logocentrism: the word as presence) and the necessity of difference. Man's choice and fate are created in man's fall into meaning.

Even though Adam and Eve catch a glimpse into the operation of language as the function of difference rather than presence, they do not remember their lesson. Their forgetfulness chains man to a system of Catch-22, because he continues to accept the a priori authority of God rather than language demystified as the true origin of his freedom. Although Adam now understands God as retribution and mercy and life as goodness and evil, he forgets that his human condition is now caught in the modality of language and is therefore created and shaped by it. As long as the first law is accepted blindly, the Catch-22s will proliferate; as long as language is seen as presence, emanating from the authority and being of God, it can be used as a weapon against man to tyrannize him.

Now we can see how Genesis and the novel implicate each other. The acceptance of the Genesis myth by a culture functions in the same way as society's acceptance of Catch-22. The laws of Genesis and Catch-22 lead men to become culprits and victims: men passively resign themselves to suffering and pain, they freely take on a burden of guilt, they do not question authority. Adherence to the law shielded Adam from knowledge and meaning, just as belief in Catch-22 screens man from recognizing the role of language as oppressor.

In Heller's novel, Yossarian comes to the realization that the way civilization uses language is a Catch-22 as long as that language pretends to presence; he comes to understand that Catch-22 has no ontology outside of its own self-reference, which (as a model) need not conform to the outside world. Yossarian liberates himself from this tyranny of language by recognizing: "Catch-22 did not exist, he was positive of that, but it made no difference. What did matter was that everyone thought it existed, and that was much worse, for there was no object or text to ridicule or refute, to accuse, criticize, attack, amend. . . ." In disbelieving Catch-22 as either "object or text," Yossarian disbelieves the word as presence, and he discredits the authority implicit in the language of logocentrism. There is no object in the text and there is no privileged text (as there supposedly is in Genesis) promulgating *absolute* law, sustaining an implacable a priori authority. Yossarian realizes the power of this fiction to hide the ugliness and brutality of human exploitation. In so doing, he sees this fiction as perversion: it represents language's power to rationalize human suffering, to condone human evil, and to create unjust, absurd laws which bind and beguile through their pretense to presence. But Yossarian would never have achieved this important epiphany without Adam's transgression against the first law back in Eden, a step, as it happens, not forgotten by the hero of Joseph Heller's novel.

In the novel, the very elements of the original temptation scene in Genesis are inverted, each action carefully replayed and parodied so that it is undone. Adam, not Eve, is the first tempted, and the temptation takes place outside the garden of Eden in the world of modern chaos. Yossarian comes to the site of the temptation, Snowden's funeral, fully informed of the knowledge of good and evil. He has flown the mission over Avignon during which Snowden lay dying, while Yossarian tried futilely to help mend the tail gunner's wounds. Yossarian learned an important lesson from Snowden's dying, a lesson deferred for the reader until the end of the novel. With Snowden's death, Yossarian comes to understand that the fragile breath of life is all that separates man from garbage. Consequently, as naked Yossarian watches Snowden being buried in a wooden box, he tells Milo Minderbinder that he is sitting in "the tree of life . . . and of knowledge of good and evil, too." His awareness of the meaning of Snowden's death is the knowledge of life itself, and, by the same token, the knowledge of good and evil as well. This awareness places Yossarian, he feels, next to Adam, the first man to know the plenitude of life at the very threshold of death.

If Yossarian sees himself as Adam, we do not have to look very far for a surrogate Satan, whom we find in the arch proponent of the excesses and corruption of the capitalistic system, Milo Minderbinder. Milo's ingenuity is undauntable and he rationalizes his corrupt business schemes with a solipsistic logic that is deceptive like Satan's. He maintains that what is good for his financial syndicate is good for everybody because everybody has a share. Of course, no one has a share, but the great deceiver lets everyone think he has. Milo is a devious chameleon with irresistible charm; he is everything to everybody: a mayor of Palermo, a knight of Malta, a mess officer, a pilot, etc.

Like his Genesis prototype, Milo is the tempter, and he tries repeatedly to tempt Yossarian into a business partnership. But Yossarian has none of the proclivities so necessary for success with Milo: Yossarian "could never win money gambling. . . . Even when he cheated he couldn't win, because the people he cheated against were always better at cheating too. There were two disappointments to which he had resigned himself: he would never be a skeet shooter, and he would never make money." Hoping Yossarian's unlimited fruit supply for his liver ailment would pertain to a joint business venture, Milo urges a partnership early in the novel, but Yossarian turns him down. A second time Milo proposes a "sure fire" scheme to cheat the Federal Government out of six thousand dollars, but Yossarian refuses again. This time Milo responds: "You're honest! You're the only one I know that I can really trust."

Consequently, when Milo needs an honest opinion he comes to Yossarian for it. Milo has cornered the market on Egyptian cotton only to find there is no demand for cotton at all. With most of his capital invested in a bumper crop he cannot unload, Milo hopes desperately to sell the cotton as candy by covering little balls of it with chocolate. He comes to Yossarian to test out his packaging idea. Milo happens to find Yossarian attending Snowden's funeral in a tree, which Milo in his pedestrian way only sees as a chestnut tree. Here, in an exact parody of Genesis, Yossarian is tempted with the fruit of corporate deception, the chocolate covered cotton. Like Christ, the second Adam, Yossarian has been tempted by Satan three times. Naïvely, Yossarian tastes of the fruit, not knowing what it is, thinking it candy, but he immediately spits it out. It tastes too bad for him to consider eating more. Adam has rejected the "mind bender" Satan. Adam can tell the difference between cotton and candy, between deception and authenticity, between the name and its meaning. He has made a fully informed choice; he has exercised his free will.

Now, in a complete reversal of Genesis, it is Yossarian, Adam the tempted, who turns to tempt the tempter. Yossarian suggests that Milo sell his cotton to the government and he provides Milo with the facile rationalizations which would make such a sale possible. The movements of the Genesis drama have been replayed completely in reverse, but with the last action, they swing to reconstruct a new paradigm. The tempted now becomes superior to the tempter. Yossarian beats Milo at his own game, rebuffing his overtures, but showing him, nonetheless, how to enmesh himself further in his own duplicitous crimes. The experience of Snowden's death has given Yossarian the moral detachment necessary to remain untouched by Milo's schemes, while Milo sinks deeper into his own deceptions, even deceiving himself with the involuted logic of Catch-22. Therefore, in the deconstructed myth, it is the new Adam who manipulates Satan into committing his own sin. In this scene, Yossarian subverts the expiation necessary for salvation in a Judeo-Christian universe, because his actions (spitting out the cotton then tempting Milo) deconstruct the gratuitous burden of original sin.

In keeping with the inverted paradigm, Heller's text poses Nately's whore as an Eve. Like Yossarian, she is a somewhat fallen figure, although she retains a marked innocence: she is innocent of the wholesome effects of a good night's sleep and, what is more, she has no knowledge of the evil and pain of death. In the original Genesis, Eve brought the knowledge of sin, i.e., death, to Adam. In Heller's novel, if we follow the process of inversion through, it is Adam who brings the news of death to Eve.

But, unlike Eve in the garden of Eden, Nately's whore screams in helpless agony at the power of death and seeks to punish the unfortunate messenger who has brought her to the realization of this fact of life. There are, surprisingly, no recriminations in the original Genesis, but in the inverted parable, Eve rebukes Adam and nearly kills him in her anger. She voices the pain and enraged resentment of all humanity before the actuality of death. The surrealistic presence of Nately's whore ever waiting in ambush to kill Yossarian, whom she mistakenly considers to be the personification of death itself, underscores the poignancy of the lesson she must continually experience in life, yet still rebels against learning.

The full implication of this replayed Genesis is apparent only at the end of the novel. Yossarian's final decision to attempt an escape to Sweden is the logical outcome of his rejection of Milo and his recognition of the nonexistence of Catch-22. The origin of man's awareness of ethical categories in the old Genesis has been replaced in the novel by an awesome awareness of man's real freedom within language. At last man is truly free to accept or reject the implications of his faith in language, and that certainly is a new beginning. The old myth is a story of the discovery of man's capacity for evil, which, however, is gratuitously presented and does not lie within man's nature. It is the story of man's servile acceptance of an a priori law and authority. The reconstruction in the novel is a story of man's acceptance of his capacity for humanity and a rejection of the law and authority under which he is always the loser. The end of the novel, viewed in light of the inverted Genesis, becomes understandable. Instead of being expelled from paradise, the modern Adam runs toward it. Sweden, like its anagram, becomes a paradisiacal haven. Yossarian "would certainly have preferred Sweden, where the level of intelligence was high and where he could swim nude with beautiful girls with low, demurring voices and sire whole happy, undisciplined tribes of illegitimate Yossarians that the state would assist through parturition and launch into life without stigma." Sweden represents a place where Yossarian as natural man would see the best in mankind prevail—high intelligence, an unselfconscious, healthy attitude toward the human body, the unlimited engendering of life: thus, generation rather than annihilation, freedom from inherited stigma, be it social or spiritual (original sin). Yossarian's flight to Sweden is the fulfillment of the quest he has pursued from the beginning of the novel: the search for life.

Unlike the original Adam who meekly leaves the garden chastened and repentant, Yossarian challenges the cosmos of Catch-22; he denies the validity behind the rules of the game. The text invokes Genesis to suggest a supplementary alternative to the first Adam's actions. On behalf of humanity, Yossarian makes the protest the first Adam might have made long ago: he refuses to be punished for actions whose consequences were not evident before; he refuses to accept the blame and guilt for his knowledge of mortality; and he refuses to be deluded by tricks of language as presence. At the end of the novel, Yossarian runs from the chaos in which the meekness and shame of the first Adam have involved mankind and tries to break into an earthly Eden. In denying the power and authority of those Catch-22 hierarchies over him, including the supposed author of this perverse cosmos, the God of tooth decay and incontinent old people, Yossarian assumes the ultimate responsibility—the management of his own life. As he tells Major Danby before he escapes: "I'm not running *away* from my responsibilities. I'm running *to* them. There's nothing negative about running away to save my life. You know who the escapists are, don't you, Danby? Not me and Orr." Yossarian maintains that those who do not confront head on the fiction of Catch-22 are the escapists.

In conclusion, if the inverted Genesis paradigm underscores the primal discontinuity between words and things, it must be stated at this point that the language of the novel as a whole by no means works for the reader, Yossarian, or its own world as if this discontinuity were always self-evident or operative. In problematizing the nature of language, Catch-22 shows that language can become reality (Mudd and Luciana are casualties of this phenomenon) and that a discontinuous language carrying a pretense of referentiality can become a facile tool of authority, self-reflexive and autotelic (the vagaries of the different meanings of sanity). In both discourses, it can wreak violence and havoc.

Nevertheless, the first Catch-22 in the Bible and all the Catch-22's in the novel operate in and through the very referentiality they displace. The novel's ironies and the ferocious bite of its satire tear at a logocentric grounding without abolishing its power. Thus, in the novel, two concepts of language continually play off each other. The Genesis paradigm is one of the many places which symbolically highlights this confrontation. The recognition of the discontinuity between words and things can only be realized in a world already asserting the ontic status of logocentrism.

Although the novel may shed light on the conditions of our use of language, it does not show us a definitive way out of our abuses. Heller's return to Genesis is significant not only as a touchstone pointing to beginnings, but also as an emblem pointing to evil itself as a human creation emanating from a belief in languages's pretenses and tricks. If logocentrism is a dangerous fiction, I do not believe that Sweden represents the efficaciousness of recognizing a discontinuous discourse. Yossarian's escape to Sweden, as I have chosen to see it, is the final act in reverse of a deconstructed myth. That this act is perhaps sentimental and that it revalorizes the first Genesis in the novel's precise inversion down to the last detail does not mitigate, however, one important fact about the ending. Yossarian's journey to Sweden is indeed open-ended, the arrival at his destination perhaps deferred forever. Instead of merely viewing this open-ended escape as the running toward another fiction, a mythic paradise, might it not be seen as a statement that Yossarian retains the right to create in the future his own discourse?

And while the philosophical issues of language raised in the novel remain unresolved, Yossarian's experience in the tree of the knowledge of good and evil projects an important theme. Yossarian's recognition of himself as a new Adam in all his humanity and mortality carries with it the existential right to be able to discover and interpret the destructiveness of discourse wherever it may be in the workings of language. This is enacted in Yossarian's rejection of the "mind bender." Hence, the novel's uncovering the space between logocentrism and its alternative, a language of discontinuity, exposes many of the processes of language which violate man's very humanity.

WALTER JAMES MILLER

Joseph Heller's Fiction

Consider a novel that has been described like this. It is fat, overlong, experimental in structure, intricate in texture. It abounds in allusions, symbols, allegory. It's surrealistic, Dadaist, absurdist, Dantean. Its message is savagely radical: it satirizes cherished notions from the value of the family to the viability of God.

Offhand you would say it sounds like an avant-garde work doomed to be admired—perhaps exegesed—by a small following. You would be unprepared to hear these additional facts. *Catch-22*, as it's called, enjoys worldwide popularity. Its author, Joseph Heller, is the greatest-selling writer of serious fiction in American history. Since *Catch-22* appeared in 1961, it has helped create such a demand for innovative fiction that America-at-large suddenly recognized another experimental writer of Heller's own generation—the long-neglected Kurt Vonnegut—and made best-sellers too out of younger innovators like Thomas Pynchon, E. L. Doctorow, and Robert Coover. Many anomalies for which *Catch-22* prepared the public include this: Heller's second and third novels—*Something Happened* (1974) and *Good as Gold* (1979)—differ so radically from the first, they could have been written by two other innovators.

How could Heller perform such a miracle: producing avant-garde art that appeals to a mass audience? He got history and humor to work hand in

From *American Writing Today*. © 1991 by Walter James Miller.

hand. In the 1960s many Americans were beginning to question the morality of Uncle Sam's military ventures in Southeast Asia. Increasingly they were doubting the wisdom, even the motives, of many business, professional, and governmental leaders. As the number of citizens suspecting that a rationalist society might be irrational grew and grew, so did the sales of *Catch-22*. Seemingly an attack on the military-industrial complex of World War II, in which Heller had flown 60 combat missions, the novel actually aims, through highly original use of anachronisms, to expose the entire power system of the postwar world. Heller even foresaw many of the emerging crises of our times. *Catch-22* provides not only a catchphrase to describe modern frustrations, but also Scripture, complete with prophecy and identification of Satan, for the new counter-culture.

But Heller's sense of timing would have availed him little, given the unorthodoxy of his approach, if he had not seduced his reader with black humor and absurdist wit. Step by step the reader braving Heller's strange terrain is rewarded with irreverent gags that promise shocking revelations. "Nately had a bad start. He came from a good family." "All over the world, young men were dying for what they had been told was their country."

Apparently Heller's own disenchantment began with his early experiences as an author. After the war he studied literature and writing at New York, Columbia, and Oxford Universities. By 1949, aged 26, already published in several leading magazines, he was regarded as one of America's most promising fiction-writers.

But then he stopped writing. For more than four years. Why? With his now well-known penchant for staring right through appearances, he came to realize that what he had learned to write—and what editors were so eager to buy—was trivial, formulaic, replicating. He turned his back on the traditional short story, with its unalloyed "realism." Its rationalist structure, its assumptions of continuity in situation and character, its neat resolutions apparently did not square with his own experiences. As soldier, university teacher, advertising writer, citizen—he's an indefatigable student of current events—he has lost confidence in surface meaning, what we smugly call cause-and-effect, determinacy. Realism photographs only outer reality. He had to find a structure and a style faithful to the absurdities he detected inside events, behind beliefs and policies.

Long immersion in the classics, from Homer to Dostoyevsky, and in innovators like Joyce and Faulkner, had not suggested any new approach he could use now. Then in 1953 his reading of Louis-Ferdinand Céline's *Journey to the End of Night* provided a leaven that made sense of Heller's literary and personal background. "Céline did things with time and structure and colloquial speech I'd never experienced before. I found those experiences pleasurable," he recalls. "It was unlike reading Joyce, who did things I'd never seen but that were not pleasurable." Art should enlighten the broadest possible audience, Heller maintains, but to do so it must also entertain. Five weeks later he was launched on a second literary career—this one genuine, continuous, self-renewing.

One reason *Catch-22* took eight years to write is that Heller had a full-time job and could invent new fictional maneuvers only by night. Another is that he felt impelled to work everything he knew, from his sensations of air combat in 1944 to his disgust with the politics of 1960, all into one cycloramic canvas.

Ostensibly, the story focuses on the exploits of the 256th Squadron, operating from the Mediterranean isle of Pianosa to bomb the Nazis' Gothic Line in Italy and installations in France. Yossarian, the main character in a cast of 60 well-defined individuals, earns a captaincy and a medal because he dared a second run over a well-armed, now fully alerted, target. But whenever he nears the number of missions he must fly to earn a tour of non-combat duty, his ambitious superiors keep raising that number far beyond the official Army requirement. They want to build up the best record of any unit. That's easier with seasoned veterans like Nately and Yossarian than with the green recruits who would replace them. Likely to die not for his country but for his colonels, finding all avenues of appeal blocked by those same commanders, Yossarian tries to escape the trap by feigning illness, even insanity. Obviously a crazy airman must be grounded. But there's a catch. He must ask to be grounded, and anyone asking to be excused from combat duty thereby proves he's not crazy. He "would be crazy to fly more missions and sane if he didn't, but if he was sane he had to fly them. If he flew them he was crazy and didn't have to; but if he didn't want to he was sane and had to." Catch-22 becomes the master symbol, its many variations representing loopholes in the law that mean the powerful can take away the rights of their fellow citizens. Realizing that the Establishment itself has become Evil Incarnate, Yossarian deserts, following a long line of American dropouts, real and fictional, who decide to obey the Higher Conscience: Henry David Thoreau, hero of his autobiographical *Civil Disobedience*, Mark Twain's Huckleberry Finn, Ernest Hemingway's Lieutenant Henry.

Actually, Heller crams into 1944-1945 telling samples of American history from the crowding of the Indians off their own land in the 1800s to the controversies rampant in the Eisenhower Administration (1953-1961). Flashbacks were old tools when Heller used them to uncover corruption in, for example, the medical profession; what was new was his technique of creating fictional events in one period of time (World War II) that parodied actual events that would not occur until a later period (the 1950s). Senator

Joseph McCarthy's 1954 anti-Communist battle cry, "Who promoted Major Peress?" is analyzed as an absurd question, "Who promoted Major Major?" Because his first name is Major, an IBM machine reads that as his rank. Heller's answer to McCarthy is typically symbolic. No one is guilty of promoting the Communist Peress; a machine, an organization operating automatically, did it. And the implications of Secretary of Defense Charles Wilson's blooper, "What's good for General Motors is good for the country and vice versa," are dramatized as Lieutenant Milo Minderbinder's black-market policy: "What's good for M & M Enterprises is good for the country." Black-market tactics become Heller's symbol for free enterprise itself; it upholds the consumer's freedom to pay high prices or starve. Some of Heller's anachronisms involve such accurate extrapolations, from conditions rampant when he was writing, that they prepared readers for life in the 1960s and 1970s: like scandals in the U.S. agricultural programs and in the Vietnam war.

Heller's overall time-structure was one of his technical experiments making humor necessary as an inducement. Soon after Yossarian sees, or thinks, of someone or something, he/Heller shies away from this experience, spiraling back over previous action, spiraling so that all events past-present-future are revealed in simultaneity. This recycling continues so long as Yossarian is at the mercy of the "spinning reasonableness" of Catch-22. But as soon as he takes definite steps to break out of the vicious cycle, the action becomes linear. Thus the novel's "story-line" resembles the path of a homing aircraft that circles an airport several times before it gets "on the beam" and flies straight in.

Shying, spiraling in the first 38 chapters determines the way, for example, Yossarian's most traumatic experience is revealed to us. Eight times he recalls the dying of Snowden, a gunner wounded over Avignon. Each time we get further details before Yossarian shies. Not until he is close to resolving his problem can he bear, in Chapter 41, to recall the entire scene. Some early readers, even some critics, missed the psychological validity behind this kind of narration. They saw instead only repetition and thought Heller inept.

Psychological reality also guides Heller when he has characters "feel" their way through crises not by thinking in words but by reliving, or reflecting on, archetypal situations. After Yossarian sabotages a mission, he copes with guilt feelings. Walking across the isle, he sees a soldier eating a pomegranate. This reminds the reader of Persephone, who lost her innocence by tasting pomegranate in Hades. Yossarian enters a forest, itself a classical symbol of descent into the shadow side of existence. In sudden darkness he's frightened by burgeoning mushrooms. We know by now that for an airman, they suggest exploding flak and so, especially since they spring here out of black Hades, death itself. Limp and pale, they suggest impotence, dread reward for him anxious over guilt. But Yossarian flees out onto the beach, a margin between two worlds, and enters the Mediterranean. In a ritual of baptism he swims until he feels clean. The scene especially signifies when we realize that Yossarian has been identified earlier, through allusions, with the protagonist of T. S. Eliot's *The Waste Land*: until now, Yossarian has feared death by water, that is, rebirth through baptism. Neither Yossarian nor the reader need verbalize these experiences as I have verbalized them here; the same symbols that work subliminally for the character work for the reader to reflect change of mood from anxiety to peace.

Yossarian "thinks" his way through another crisis while sitting naked in a tree, where Milo visits him. Through a combination of Yossarian's remarks, our own associations, and the chaplain's reflections on this tableau, we see Yossarian as Jesus on the cross and Adam at the tree, Milo the businessman as Satan.

Even characters whom we know only from the outside develop in terms of allusion and allegory. Since Major de Coverley's first name is never pronounced, we suspect he represents divinity; in some religions God's name is unutterable. But inevitably we think of a famous prude in English literature, Sir Roger de Coverley, and we find the name apt for the major. "*Roger*" is an Air Force code word for "*Received and understood.*" To "roger" a woman means, in British slang, to have one's will of her; this resonates with ironies in Heller's overall situation.

Alerted that Heller characterizes through tag-names, we quickly grasp the nature of Nately (natally, suggesting newly-born, innocent, conscious of genealogy), of Luciana (who brings light into Yossarian's room), of Wintergreen (survival is his talent). Alerted that Heller describes through cultural allusions, we understand characters like Milo and Dobbs all the better if we recognize certain lines about them as parodies of Eliot, Whitman, Tennyson, Shakespeare.

Heller achieves his most memorable effects through surrealistic or expressionistic distortion. Since Milo's black-market operations are international in scope, they inevitably ally him with his counterparts in the Nazi war machine. These dealings take priority over declared national policies; as part of his "contracts" with the Germans, Milo bombs his own squadron. A congressional investigation clears him once he proves the transaction made a tidy profit for free enterprise. Heller thus dramatizes what he sees as the truth behind international cartels. They make a mockery of patriotism; they aid the enemy; businessmen may use the chaos of war to increase their power over (to fight) their own people. Heller's hospital scenes include a man so completely bandaged that no one has ever seen, heard, or touched the person inside. He seems to represent the *thing* that war reduces a man to. Or is the Soldier in White some sinister listening apparatus? Heller intensifies the nightmare quality of surreal situations by alternating them with realistic narration. For sheer descriptive power, metaphoric intensity, and poetic cadences, his realistic battle scenes are unsurpassed in the literature of war.

Catch-22, then, shows the individual in the clutches of monolithic organizations like armies, cartels, governments. Heller's next two novels deal with variations on the same theme. But they differ in that Heller gives greater attention to family relations as intermediate between the individual and his organization, and he popularizes other avant-garde techniques that suit his new situations.

In *Something Happened* Robert Slocum, a minor executive, gropes for status in the dark labyrinths of a giant corporation. Again, the struggle for power within the organization (army, corporation) consumes more energy than does the struggle to achieve the organization's declared goals (winning a war, serving the customer). While Yossarian ultimately rejects any deal that forces him to collaborate with cynical leaders, Slocum learns to play the power game, accepting its hypocrisies, treacheries, unremitting anxieties. Slocum learns by practising on his family. If the British say that the Battle of Waterloo was won on the playing fields of Eton College, then Heller seems to say that the Battle of Corporate Success is won on the testing-grounds of the patriarchal household. Slocum uses any tactic necessary to manipulate his wife, children, and mother, keeping human relations at a distance so he can concentrate on "real" goals: for example, to be the man who makes a three-minute speech at the company's annual convention.

One of his sons sweetly dramatizes an alternative way of life. A superb runner, the boy has no trouble staying ahead of his competitors. But he hates competition and likes to be with people, so when he's running, for the sheer joy of it, he often waits for the others to catch up to him! By degrees, the system, represented by the school track-coach, and ultimately the father too must crush this deviant—that is, humane—child.

Snuffing out a child, who represents man's future with his hope for integrity regained, is part of continuously symbolic action. Slocum has so little sense of self, he takes on characteristics of the person he's with; his wife knows he's been with Kagle if Slocum comes home limping like Kagle. Again, tag-names signify. Executives are named Green, Black, White, Brown; Gray figures near the end. Slocum's other son, an autistic child, prefers lifeless objects, mechanical sameness. Named Derek, connoting "derrick," he serves as an extension of one aspect of his father.

Here Heller's technique is so daring, it's no exaggeration to say that only the author of *Catch-22* could have risked it. His audience had learned to trust his experiments. In order to focus on the dehumanized, obsessed but tranquilized state of mind of a character who, to paraphrase Coleridge, must rise as the condition of not falling, Heller gives us nothing but Slocum's interior monologue. And that monologue is flat, monotonous, dogged, paranoiac. Two passages will illustrate not only the even, drily arithmetic style; they show too the parallels between Slocum's family life and corporate life, the way his need to control is based on fear engendered by hierarchism. On page 17 Slocum thinks: "In my department, there are six people who are afraid of me, and one small secretary who is afraid of all of us. I have one other person working for me who is not afraid of anyone, not even me, and I would fire him quickly, but I'm afraid of him." On page 355, Slocum thinks: "In the family in which I live there are four people of whom I am afraid. Three of these four people are afraid of me, and each of these three is also afraid of the other two. Only one member of the family is not afraid of any of the others, and that one is an idiot."

Not even Kafka would risk using such Kafkaesque techniques for 500 pages without relief. But Heller succeeds in getting the reader to agree that small samples no longer suffice. If such conditions pervade our culture, then art depicting them may defeat its purpose unless it haunts us with equal pertinacity.

In *Good as Gold* Heller continues to study the links between person, family, and gigantic organization. In addition to devising a new novelistic structure, he invents a new way of studying character and again blends realism with black humor and surrealism. Professor Gold is something of a cross between Slocum and Yossarian. Like Slocum, Gold wants to rise—this time, it's in the government—and for most of the novel, he is willing, like Slocum, to sacrifice family, friends, his humanity. But unlike Slocum, when Gold finally faces the question "How much lower would he have to crawl to rise to the top?" he turns his back on the abyss and rejoins family, profession, heritage. Like Yossarian, he first considers joining the power elite but then flees it. Like the airman and unlike the business executive, the professor is brilliant, so Heller is free once again to use his towering talents as a wit.

But Gold is more than a new combination of options open to an individual poised on a low rung in the hierarchy. He's an original study of the way a citizen may choose a national celebrity as his model for success. Jewish Professor Gold decides he will "out-Kissinger" Kissinger, who rose from Harvard professor to become the first Jewish U.S. Secretary of State. The more Gold imitates what (he thinks) Kissinger had to do to get to the top, the more Gold hates Kissinger and Gold. Gold's analysis of Kissinger's character helps Gold change his own. Heller develops a new form of satire: he criticizes a public figure by studying someone who imitates him. He concludes that such leaders are not worthy to serve as role models for anyone with a spark of conscience. Our leaders serve as models of what not to follow.

Gold lives with his wife and children, visits other relatives, and teaches in New York. The New York side of Gold's life Heller handles with satiric realism. Because Gold's review of the President's book *My Year in the White House* pleases the White House, Gold commutes on weekends to Washington hoping to attain a major government post. Gold's Washington side—serving on a commission, having an affair with the daughter of a powerful but anti-Semitic public figure—Heller handles as surrealism. Near the crisis he blends the two settings, two modes. A surrealistic situation that Gold's complicated life might well create in Washington is superimposed on his realistic experiences as he jogs around a track in New York.

In this book Heller especially exploits the sentence that undoes its own work. Its syntax symbolizes the double talk of the public official. "All of us," a White House aide tells Gold, "want you working with us as soon as possible after the people above us decide whether they want you working here at all. . . . In Washington, . . . you rise quickly and can't fall very far. . . . Do whatever you want as long as you do whatever we want. We have no ideas, and they're pretty firm. . . . This administration will back you all the way until it has to."

Fidelity to his subject matter leads Heller to adopt a different method for each novel. Still, I hope he someday spirals back to the consistently multi-level approach of what remains his greatest work: *Catch-22*. This could occur naturally. I think the complex combination of black humor with allegory, symbolism, and allusion, which makes his first novel a work of Dantean dimension, occurred to Heller as a summational approach. As he once said, "Everything I knew at the time is in *Catch-22*." Surely he will sometime feel the need for another encyclopedic synthesis of everything he "knows." For that, he may well have to circle back and around before coming in for a landing.

SANFORD PINSKER

Catch-22

For Heller a novel generally begins not with a structure, an intricate plan or "plot" to be worked out, but with a sentence, one that simply popped into his head and then rattled around there, haunting him. *Catch-22* begins not only in medias res—in the middle of things—but also in something akin to wonderment: "It was love at first sight." Heller's readers often feel the same way; they fall in love with the novel's playful sense of the absurd, with the way Yossarian shapes up as a rebel out to outfox the system.

Readers first meet Heller's aviator-protagonist in the infirmary rather than the wild blue yonder. Yossarian is afflicted by a pain in his liver that falls "short of being jaundice" but at the same time is sufficiently puzzling to require extended hospitalization. Presumably the doctors could deal with jaundice, and they could certainly return him to active duty if it were *not* jaundice, but "this just being short of jaundice all the time confused them." To the military bureacracy Yossarian's liver is both a puzzlement and an aggravation; and as the novel unfolds, the same things might be said of Yossarian himself.

Nothing, of course, unsettles rigid bureaucratic minds more than an aberration lodging stubbornly "between the cracks" and just beyond the grip of rules. Yossarian's case of near-jaundice is a tiny example; Yossarian himself is a much larger one. He spends as much time as possible in the hospital, not

From *Understanding Joseph Heller.* © 1991 by the University of South Carolina.

only because the meals are better there or because he can flirt with the nurses, but mostly because there he is *safe*.

Yossarian enters the world of his novel knowing what the protagonists of earlier war novels such as Erich Maria Remarque's *All Quiet on the Western Front* (1929) or Ernest Hemingway's *A Farewell to Arms* (1929) soon discover; namely, that the life of a combat soldier is nasty, brutish, and likely to be very, very short. Heller's protagonist has even fewer illusions about the patriotic rhetoric of recruitment posters or about the "romantic" character of war. He seeks out pockets of safety because he wants, above all else, to survive. As he tells Clevinger, a character whose principles are matched only by the mindless passion with which he holds them, "They're trying to kill me." Not surprisingly, Clevinger, who points out that "they're shooting at *everyone*," concludes that Yossarian is "crazy." Clevinger's opinion is widely shared by those who come to hate and fear Yossarian's increasingly desperate efforts to survive; for them war is not only necessary but, more important, also perfectly sane, and those who throw monkey wrenches into its bureaucratic machinery must by definition be crazy.

Indeed, *crazy* is one of the novel's "charged words," symptomatic of a world neatly divided into the one character (Yossarian) whose sanity renders him suspect and the others whose versions of craziness are regarded as sane. Smiling down on such a world—one in which aerial photographs of "tight bombing clusters" count for more than hits or misses, or where a precision drill team has its hands surgically removed so that their commanding officer can shout "Look . . . No hands!" as they swing past in parade review—is, of course, the overarching absurdity of Catch-22 itself:

> There was only one catch and that was Catch-22, which specified that a concern for one's own safety in the face of dangers that were real and immediate was the process of a rational mind. Orr was crazy and could be grounded. All he had to do was ask; and as soon as he did, he would no longer be crazy and would have to fly more missions. Orr would be crazy to fly more missions and sane if he didn't, but if he was sane he had to fly them. If he flew them he was crazy and didn't have to; but if he didn't want to he was sane and had to. Yossarian was moved very deeply by the absolute simplicity of this clause of Catch-22 and let out a respectful whistle.
>
> "That's some catch, that Catch-22," he observed.
> "It's the best there is," Doc Daneeka agreed.

Granted, this is akin to the "logic" that reigns in Lewis Carroll's *Alice in*

Wonderland rather than in conventional war novels, but that is precisely
Heller's point: wars can no longer be described as "hell"; they are irrational,
absurd, and in most important respects differ very little from the
bureaucratic life citizens and employees experience regularly in peacetime.
War merely writes the lessons of Catch-22 in starker print.

Paul Fussell's recent nonfiction book *Wartime* (1989) suggests that
there may have been more affinities between Heller's art and the "real war"
than many had realized. The usual line of argument about *Catch-22* (one
often encouraged by Heller himself) was that World War II, its ostensible
subject, is a veiled metaphor for first the Vietnam war and then for the larger
absurdities of the military-industrial complex. Perhaps so, but as Fussell
points out, the "truth" about World War II—as it was lived in the foxholes
and reflected in memoirs—is not at variance with his research. As he argues:

> What was it about the Second World War that moved the
> troops to constant verbal subversion and contempt? What was it
> that made the Americans, especially, so fertile with insult and
> cynicism, calling women Marines BAMS (broad-assed Marines)
> and devising SNAFU, with its offspring TARFU ("Things are
> really fucked up"), FUBAR ("Fucked up beyond all recognition")
> and perhaps less satisfying FUBB ("Fucked up beyond belief")?
> It was not just the danger and fear, the boredom and uncertainty
> and loneliness and deprivation. It was the conviction that
> optimistic publicity and euphemism had rendered their
> experience so falsely that it would never be readily
> communicable. They knew that in its representation to the laity,
> what was happening to them was systematically sanitized and
> Norman Rockwellized, not to mention Disneyfied.

Yossarian, then, is the man who tries desperately to bring his brand of
"good news"—and a sense of Fussell's "truth"—to those still dwelling in the
darkness of Plato's cave. His curious name earmarks him as an outsider and
a potentially subversive character. Heller initially imagined Yossarian as an
Assyrian, someone even more marginal, historically and culturally, than the
Jew who generally fulfills this role in traditional war novels—only to discover
later that Yossarian is an Armenian name. No matter, however, for *Yossarian*
sticks in one's memory, rather like his unpredictable behaviors stick in the
craw of his superiors.

Yossarian is simultaneously an enigma and an Everyman, the rebel
whose bizarre behaviors unsettle and a thoroughly representative figure of
the soldier's plight. What gives him both distinction and style, however, are

the comic lengths to which he will go to pursue the folly of his version of the truth. For example, Yossarian's idea of a good joke is to write letters to everyone he knows telling them that he is going on a dangerous mission: "'They asked for volunteers. It's very dangerous, but someone has to do it. I'll write you the instant I get back.' And he had not written anyone since." Forced to censor the letters of enlisted men while he is confined to the hospital, Yossarian soon discovers that their lives are only slightly more interesting than his and that the chore is as monotonous as it is boring. So he gives his task a darkly imaginative twist, one emblematic of what might be called the Yossarian syndrome:

> To break the monotony he invented games. Death to all modifiers, he declared one day, and out of every letter that passed through his hands went every adverb and every adjective. The next day he made war on articles. He reached a much higher plane of creativity the following day when he blacked out everything in the letters but *a*, *an*, and *the*. That erected more dynamic intralinear tensions, he felt, and in just about every case left a message far more universal.

No doubt there are contemporary literary critics who would insist that Yossarian's linguistic games speak to the capacity of language to cancel itself out, indeed, to the impossibility of meaning itself. And other critics, more persuaded by the tragic rhythms of history, would remind Heller that World War II—Fussell's study notwithstanding—was waged to halt the spread of fascism's ugliest, most inhuman face. In *Catch-22* boredom is a bigger enemy than the Nazis; social critics are not likely to agree either with Heller's assessment or with his moral judgment.

Yossarian, of course, sees his games as versions of protest, as efforts—however minuscule, however desperate, however ineffectual—to assert the claims of the individual against those of the Machine. Given the excesses stacked on the side of the latter, it is hardly surprising that there should be a certain amount of excess on behalf of the former. Indeed, *Catch-22* thrives on excess (perhaps too much so), and this includes Yossarian's efforts to gum up semiofficial communications. Those in the know—e.g., ex-PFC Wintergreen—know better; they chuck those memos that strike them as "prolix" into the wastebaskets and thus end up wielding more *real* power than the officially powerful. By contrast Yossarian is simply playful. For example, in one letter he blacks out everything but its salutation, "Dear Mary," and then adds a closing of his own design: "I yearn for you tragically. A. T. Tappman, Chaplain, U.S. Army." Chaplain Tappman strikes Yossarian's ear as having a nice ring. Other pen names appeal to him because he can alternate the position of first and last name, as is the case with Washington Irving and Irving Washington. Washington Irving, the author of *The Sketch Book of Geoffrey Crayon, Gent.*, is one of those names that students of American literary history must dutifully remember. But he is more widely recognized as the author of "Rip Van Winkle" and "The Legend of Sleepy Hollow," two of *The Sketch Book*'s most famous pieces and early examples of what would become a staple ingredient of American humor—the tall tale.

Catch-22 is filled with stretchers and leg-pulls, with outrageous yarns told in poker face. What else is the saga of the LePage Glue Gun (which can ominously attach a whole squadron of fighter planes together and thus bring them crashing to the ground) but a yarn in the best tradition of the Old Southwest? And where else could a single aviator's moans (during a briefing) turn so contagious, eventually rising to a deafening, collective crescendo? The rub, of course, is that Yossarian's superiors take their absurdities seriously. They confuse the fatuous with the profound, but Heller's readers— as beneficiaries of the dramatic ironies he so generously heaps up—do not. Thus, Colonel Cargill, a man who has singlehandedly raised the cliché to new dizzying heights, puts it this way: "Men. . . . You're American officers. The officers of no other army in the world can make that statement. Think about it." Heller's readers do, and split their sides laughing.

Meanwhile, Heller provides this deadpan account of Cargill's absurd biography, presumably by way of explaining how he came to speak as he does:

> Colonel Cargill, General Peckem's troubleshooter, was a forceful, ruddy man. Before the war he had been an alert, hard-hitting, aggressive marketing executive. Colonel Cargill was so awful a marketing executive that his services were much sought after by firms eager to establish losses for tax purposes. Throughout the civilized world from Battery Park to Fulton Street, he was known as a dependable man for a fast tax write-off. . . . Colonel Cargill could be relied on to run the most prosperous enterprise into the ground. He was a self-made man who owed his lack of success to nobody.

Such minor characters (there are dozens of them) give *Catch-22* its peculiar flavor—its bulk, its texture, its richness. Many are introduced by quick brushstrokes of biography akin to the profiles that appear regularly in John Dos Passos' *USA* trilogy, but Heller throws in so many curve balls, so many absurdist contradictions, that the result is laughter. Like most great humorists, his premises are disarmingly simple (in this case he turns clichés on their heads so that Colonel Cargill starts at the top and works his way down), but his extended executions are verbally brilliant. Here, for example, is how he introduces Clevinger, a character so smart, so believing, so much the Boy Scout, that he is a dope:

> As a Harvard undergraduate he had won prizes in scholarship for just about everything, and the only reason he had not won prizes in scholarship for everything else was that he was too busy signing petitions, circulating petitions and challenging petitions, joining discussion groups and resigning from discussion groups, attending youth congresses, picketing other youth congresses and organizing student committees in defense of dismissed faculty members. Everyone agreed that Clevinger was certain to go far in the academic world. In short, Clevinger was one of those people with lots of intelligence and no brains, and everyone knew it except those who soon found it out.

Subsequent biographies in *Catch-22* are cut from the same absurdist cloth that gave us Colonel Cargill. Major Major's father, for example, is a rural variant of the same something-out-of-nothing philosophy that worked with such perverse efficiency in big business. Here the business is farming or, more precisely, *not* farming:

> The government paid him well for every bushel of alfalfa he did not grow. The more alfalfa he did not grow, the more money the government gave him, and he spent every penny he didn't earn on new land to increase the amount of alfalfa he did not produce. Major Major's father worked without rest at not growing alfalfa.

And the same essential technique, the same tired joke, reemerges as Heller sets about chronicling the saga of the AmerIndian as emblematically represented in Chief Halfoat's doomed family:

> "Every place we pitched our tent, [Chief Halfoat wails] they sank an oil well. Every time they sank a well, they hit oil. And every time they hit oil, they made us pack up our tent and go someplace else. We were human divining rods. Our whole family had a natural affinity for petroleum deposits, and soon every oil company in the world had technicians chasing us around."

As his name suggests, Chief Halfoat is half social commentary, half *schlemiel*; his fate is his bad luck, and his bad luck is his fate. Granted, Heller hardly expects readers to belabor what he presents with the broad strokes of farce. What profit is there in grinding fine what is patently true about American history?

At the same time, however, Heller's sociopolitical agenda is clear, and those who laugh do so knowing full well that they have numbered themselves on the side of the angels. Indeed, in each case Heller's exaggerated portraits drive toward general (and easy) social truths—about the seemingly intelligent who are hopelessly befuddled, about those who turn government subsidies into windfalls, about the continuing exploitation, and stereotyping, of native Americans. Put another way, his platoon on Pianosa may have been served up as a microcosm of a larger American society, but Heller—unlike, say, the Norman Mailer of *The Naked and the Dead*—is more interested in a novel of comic energy than in a novel of Ideas. The result is a version of literary cartooning—one-dimensional portraits designed more with caricature than fully rounded characterization in mind: a Colonel Korn who delivers "corny" speeches to his troops, an Aarfy who is likened to the stylized bark of a friendly dog (in cartoons, invariably rendered as "Awrf, awrf!"), a Major —— de Coverley whose blank represents the enigma he is, and an Orr who will ultimately come to represent an alternative (an "or") to a world divided into the absurdist deaths represented, and justified, by Catch-22 and the survival signified by going AWOL. Moreover, Heller uses the leitmotifs of tag-lines and distinctive clothing to peg his minor characters: Doc Daneeka responds to every crisis by whining, "You think you've got problems? What about me?" while Aarfy is never far from his pipe or McWatt from his red pajamas.

Given the bulk of Heller's novel, repetition figures both as a strategy and at times as a liability. It is, after all, one thing to introduce Major Major's father as a "sober God-fearing man whose idea of a good joke was to lie about his age" and to repeat virtually the same comic formula with regard to Doc Daneeka ("Doc Daneeka was a very neat, clean man whose idea of a good time was to sulk"). That those reporting to sick call with temperatures below 102 "had their gums and toes painted with gentian violet solution and were given a laxative to throw away into the bushes" makes its point better as a single-shot comment than as the running gag it, in fact, becomes. In short, repetition runs rampant in *Catch-22*.

At one point, for example, a character announces that he sees "everything twice" and the condition instantly becomes widespread; at another point much the same thing occurs to those with "flies in their eyes."

Even the title of the novel—which was originally "Catch-18," but was changed to avoid confusion with the (then) more popular Leon Uris's forthcoming novel, *Mila 18*—seems exactly right for the doubled, and doubling, world it describes. By doubling the number 2, Heller tightens the noose around a world where soldiers "see everything twice" and thus throw hospital wards into a panic. But that much said, even an appeal to excess cannot either explain or justify some of the verbal highjinks in *Catch-22*. Given its wide range of wit and self-indulgence (everything from the sophomoric prank to the erudite graduate school allusion), how could it?

Repetition is also at the very heart of whatever structure Heller's chaotic novel might have. The much hinted-at, long-postponed, absolutely crucial confrontation with Snowden (yet another character whose name suggests his fate) may be the book's "deep image," the dark figure in its wacky, comic carpet; but as the freezing "Snowden of yesteryear" who perished during the mission over Avignon, the moment of illumination simply won't hold up under some 450 pages of the novel's accumulated weight. "I'm cold . . . I'm cold," Snowden keeps repeating, and finally Yossarian discovers a truth truer than the justifications for war outlined on recruiting posters, truer even than the powerful absurdist grip of Catch-22 itself:

> Yossarian bent forward to peer and saw a strangely colored stain seeping through the coveralls just above the armhole of Snowden's flak suit. . . . [He] ripped open the snaps of Snowden's flak suit and heard himself scream wildly as Snowden's insides slithered down to the floor in a soggy pile and just kept dripping out. A chunk of flak more than three inches big had shot into his other side just underneath the arm and blasted all the way through, drawing whole mottled quarts of Snowden along with it through the gigantic hole in his ribs it made as it blasted out. . . .
>
> He felt goose pimples clacking all over him as he gazed down despondently at the grim secret Snowden had spilled all over the messy floor. It was easy to read the message in his entrails. Man was matter, that was Snowden's secret. Drop him out of a window and he'll fall. Set fire to him and he'll burn. Bury him and he'll rot like other kinds of garbage. The spirit gone, man is garbage. That was Snowden's secret. Ripeness was all.

Small wonder that Yossarian "circles around" this scene, half suppressing its grisly import, half attracted to its powerful image. But however much he fills in his post-Avignon days by hiding out in the infirmary or by essentially futile gestures of protest (railing at "enemies" out to kill him, moving the bombing line over Bologna, appearing buck naked at a dress parade), he cannot avoid its truth. The point is worth belaboring because some critics have made the coherence, or lack of coherence, in the novel's structure a matter of great import. Most reviewers were content to bathe the novel in adjectives (as one put it, *Catch-22* is a "wild, moving, shocking, hilarious, raging, exhilarating, giant roller-coaster of a book") and leave well enough alone; and most readers were simply overwhelmed by Heller's dazzling verbal *shpritz* (spray)—that is, the rapid-fire piling up of one hilarious episode after another. For such readers the novel was, in a word, *funny*.

However, one measure of the novel's acceptance by the academic community were the painstaking attempts—alas, often contradictory, as it turned out—to demonstrate that the apparent randomness in *Catch-22* was largely an illusion and that the novel had a structure, even a "deep meaning," that its casual readers had missed. In one of the pioneering efforts to find structure where others saw only chaos, Jan Solomon argues that "the most significant aspect of the structure of *Catch-22* is its chronology":

> The major part of the novel, focused on Yossarian, moves forward and back from a pivotal point in time. . . . Yossarian's time is punctuated, if not ordered, by the inexorable increases in the number of missions and by the repetitious returns to the relative safety and sanity of the hospital where "they couldn't dominate Death . . . but they certainly made her behave."
>
> While the dominant sequence of events shifts back and forth from the present to the past creating any period of time as equally present, equally immediate, a counter-motion controls the time of the history of Milo Minderbinder. Across the see-saw pattern of events in the rest of the novel Minderbinder moves directly forward from one success to the next.

Solomon's point is that there is a difference between the *illusion* of randomness and mere randomness, between the absurdities a writer consciously creates and those that happen, willy-nilly, in the world. Doug Gaukroger might agree about Heller's art, but in an article seeking to establish *Catch-22*'s structure of time, he argues that Solomon's thesis about mutual, and contradictory, chronologies, simply won't hold up under close inspection. For example,

> If one assumes that Milo's career did not begin until after he first met Yossarian at the time when Colonel Cathcart was demanding

45 missions, then two events (the missing morphine over Avignon, and Snowden's funeral), both of which involve a wealthy Milo in some way, are rendered chronologically impossible because they occur prior to the time of the 45 missions. . . . Excluding the fact that one cannot prove that Yossarian first met Milo at the time of 45 missions (when Yossarian had 38 missions), a large number of other events involve Milo before this time. If only two events were out of time, as has been suggested [in Solomon's article], a case might be made for a dual time scheme; however *all* the events involving Milo occurred at a time prior to the period of 45 missions.

Gaukroger's caveats need to be taken seriously (although perhaps not in the overly earnest way he goes about trying to put the novel into chronological order); nonetheless, there is merit to Solomon's general argument. After all, Yossarian circles around and/or weaves in and out of the crucial scene over Avignon in roughly the same way that Faulkner tells the tale of the rise and fall of Thomas Sutpen's "grand design" in *Absalom, Absalom*. Indeed, Yossarian's zigzagging motions—evidenced in the ways he takes evasive action or engages in fruitless debates at the hospital—identify him like a thumbprint. He means to obliterate the past he experienced over Avignon by living in a continual, and undifferentiated, present tense.

At the same time, however, Gaukroger is clearly right when he argues on behalf of a single chronology, one tied to the number of bombing missions. If Yossarian remains—or perhaps *tries* to remain—static, the number of required missions do not. Therefore, one can establish something like a rough "chronology" of the novel's plot line by paying close attention to the number of missions required before military personnel can be sent home. Generally speaking, the number escalates in integers of fives, and has a nasty habit of being raised just when Yossarian nearly reaches the magic number.

In this sense the bombing missions—whether they be relatively safe "milk runs" or more dangerous affairs—have the look of futile circles (pilots leave their base at Pianosa and return there, thus completing the circle) and cannot help but remind readers of "the soldier in white," the ghoulish study in plaster and gauze, tubes, and interchangeable jars that Yossarian met in the novel's opening pages. What the images share, of course, is a deep sense of futility. In what ways do their meaningless bombing runs differ from the enigmatic soldier in white with a zinc pipe attached to his groin and a feeding tube sewn into the bandages at his elbows? After all, "when the jar on the floor was full, the jar feeding his elbow was empty, and the two were simply switched quickly so that stuff could drip back into him"; and when a flyer nearly reaches the required number of bombing missions, he finds that they have been raised.

By contrast, the tentacles of Milo Minderbinder's ever-expanding empire move in precisely the chronological lines that Solomon suggests. Milo is a study in free enterprise capitalism—with an emphasis on the "free"—and a specialist in the art of the deal. It all begins, as many things do, with an egg. Because Milo Minderbinder controls a vital piece of information—namely, where an enterprising young man can buy an inexhaustible supply of fresh eggs for five cents apiece—and because officers have an equally inexhaustible appetite for fresh eggs, the twenty-seven-year-old wheeler-dealer finds himself earning a barracks promotion to mess officer. Thus is an entrepreneur, and a monster, born. Soon the smell of fresh eggs cooking became virtually indistinguishable from the sweet smell of Milo's success:

> In the beginning General Dreedle devoured all his meals in Milo's mess hall. Then the other three squadrons in Colonel Cathcart's group turned their mess halls over to Milo and gave him an airplane and a pilot each so that he could buy fresh eggs and fresh butter for them too. Milo's planes shuttled back and forth seven days a week as every officer in the four squadrons began devouring fresh eggs in an insatiable orgy of fresh-egg eating. General Dreedle devoured fresh eggs for breakfast, lunch and dinner—between meals he devoured more fresh eggs—until Milo located abundant sources of fresh veal, beef, duck, baby lamb chops, mushroom caps, broccoli, South African rock lobster tails, shrimp, hams, puddings, grapes, ice cream, strawberries, and artichokes.

To be sure, Milo's flimflamming empire can be written down in a single word: profiteering. But as Milo might well insist, what could possibly be more American, more democratic, than M&M Enterprise, a syndicate in which everyone owns shares and everyone shares in the profit? Moreover, isn't capitalism—both as economic system and individual possibility—what our military forces are fighting to protect? No matter that Milo engineers such outrageous barters that he ends up cornering the market on Egyptian cotton and tries to fob it off, chocolate-covered, onto the troops as food, or, worse, that he can work as easily with the enemy—orchestrating deadly raids that will presumably "benefit" both sides financially—as he does with the commodities market. Milo belongs in the great tradition of amoral Old

Southwestern horse traders that Faulkner drew upon when he had Flem Snopes amble into Jefferson, Mississippi, looking for opportunity.

Heller, of course, clearly means Milo to be one of *Catch-22*'s more insidious villains, but he also intends that he be painted with very different stripes than the bumbling fools who greedily devour his eggs without a clue as to how he can buy eggs for seven cents apiece, sell them for five cents apiece, and still turn a handsome profit. *That*, as they say, requires a certain amount of perverse genius. But Milo understands the bureaucratic mind in all its rigidity and lack of imagination—how if the army has always gotten eggs from Malta, inertia argues that the army always will. He also understands the advantages of being the "middle man" on both ends of an arrangement, and the ways in which he can take his cut as buyer *and* seller. Add the happy circumstance of being in a business with virtually no overhead (e.g., an unlimited supply of military aircraft ensures that transportation costs will never upset Milo's delicate apple cart) and the result is a subsidized venture beyond even the wildest dreams of Major Major's father.

At bottom, of course, Milo knows the truth on which all scams depend; namely, that you can't cheat an honest man. In this case, the greed he appeals to is as simple, as innocent, as an egg. Milo simply offers hungry officers the chance to buy eggs at five cents each, and the temptation proves too great to resist. The rest of his empire-building is simply history, a line on a bar graph pointing ever upward.

Soloman's thesis about the crisscrossing chronologies of Yossarian and Milo raises an interesting point, for Yossarian is a man who continually circles past the very lessons that might save him. Milo is such an instructor, albeit one who would argue that greed and survival are inextricably connected. Heller's tone makes it clear that Milo's "patriotism" is the last refuge of the profiteering scoundrel, and that the elaborate mess hall meals ultimately cost wounded fliers the first-aid supplies they badly need. In short, there are no free eggs, much less free lunches.

Given Yossarian's elaborate efforts to find a safe haven, it is curious that he so badly misses the point of Milo's one-man operation. Granted, Yossarian has a playful streak readers admire, and laugh at, but Milo knows how to build job security into what can only be called a risky business. First, he volunteers—yea, even begs—to be given combat duty. As he puts it, "Sir, I want to get in there and fight like the rest of the fellows. That's what I'm here for. I want to win medals, too."

Milo, of course, realizes that Colonel Cathcart just might take him at his word (which, after all, would not be surprising in one as thickheaded, as literal-minded, as Cathcart), but that too is part of Milo's "grand design." Thus, when Colonel Cathcart agrees, and intimates that he'll have Major

Major assign him "to the next sixty-four missions so that [he] can have seventy, too," Milo springs his trap. He is only too happy to fly combat missions, but "someone will have to begin running the syndicate for me right away. It's very complicated, and I might get shot down at any time."

The premise thus established, Milo then launches into an "explanation" so entangled, so complicated, so absurd, and of course so funny, that the technique has come to seem Heller's trademark. It begins innocently enough "Begin with a salt-free diet for General Peckem and a fat-free diet for General Dreedle," but builds by slow integers into a juggernaut of global proportions. Included are deals involving the cedars of Lebanon, peas on the high seas, galvanized zinc and Spanish *naranjas*, and as the last, exasperating straw, the Piltdown Man.

> "And—oh, yes. Don't forget Piltdown Man."
> "Piltdown Man?"
> "Yes, Piltdown Man. The Smithsonian Institution is not in a position at this time to meet our price for a second Piltdown Man, but they are looking forward to the death of a wealthy and beloved donor and. . . ."

In a world where individuals are usually characterized as replaceable units, as mere cogs in the Big Machine, Milo has engineered an elaborate, impossibly entangled way of preserving his turf. *Nobody*, the dazed Cathcart soon realizes, could possibly keep all those deals—everything from peas on the high seas to the Piltdown Man—in his head, and nobody but Milo could possibly keep M&M Enterprises afloat. Needless to say, Cathcart is forced to say what Milo has wanted to hear all along; namely, that "you can't fly sixty-four more missions. You can't even fly one more mission." Cathcart is insistent about this, and after all, Cathcart is a colonel. Milo, in short, plays men in much the same way that he manipulates the market—by using the system instead of bucking it, by finding the logical flaw, and saving loophole, in Catch-22's deadly fabric.

By contrast, Yossarian—naked and hiding in a tree after the horror of watching Snowden die—is the very typology of Innocence: Adam and Christ conflated into a single riveting, altogether disturbing image. But while Yossarian may rattle the Colonel Cathcart who lists him among his "black eyes," Yossarian's protests have a "self-evident," commonsensical smack about them that clearly scores points with readers but none with those who live under the shadow of Catch-22. In this sense Yossarian is something of a latter-day Diogenes, desperately searching Pianosa for an honest man.

Meanwhile the casualty list continues to mount, and in increasingly absurdist ways. Some, like Clevinger, fly into a cloud and never return; others are simply "disappeared." And sometimes one grotesque death leads to a chain reaction of deadly absurdities. This is precisely the case when Kid Sampson "leaped clownishly up" to touch the wing of a plane as its pilot playfully buzzed the beach. Suddenly, "something happened"—as Heller will put it ominously in his next novel—and an "arbitrary gust of wind or minor miscalculation of McWatt's senses dropped the speeding plane down just low enough for a propellor to slice him [Kid Sampson] half away." At such moments most writers draw the curtain and close off the scene. Heller, however, tends to think of the grotesque as operating on the domino principle, one dark event toppling inevitably into another and another and another. What begins as a landscape rendered in the pastels of innocence (flyers and nurses enjoying a bit of rest-and-recreation at the beach) moves by slow increments to a scene etched in layers of thick black pigment. But, for Yossarian, intimations of mortality were *always* there, even as the others frolicked and the enticing Nurse Duckett did her best to coax him out of his funk and into the company of merrymakers:

> He was haunted and tormented by the vast, boundless ocean. He wondered mournfully, as Nurse Duckett buffed her nails, about all the people who had died under water. There were surely more than a million already. . . . He peered at the vaporous Italian skyline and thought of Orr. Clevinger and Orr. Where had they gone?

And so Yossarian desperately stares at nature, looking for "signs"—not in quite the way that our Puritan founders understood Providence, but as the brooding, Hamletlike character he is. Nonetheless, Yossarian was prepared for any morbid shock, any manifestation of God's divine, and possibly terrible, plan, except for the darkly comic lesson that McWatt accidently provides.

At eye level what the shocked groundlings see are "Kid Sampson's two pale, skinny legs, still joined by strings somehow at the bloody truncated hips, standing stock-still on the raft for what seemed a full minute or two before they toppled over backward into the water"; meanwhile, McWatt's plane circles the beach slowly and begins to climb. "Who's in the plane?" Yossarian asks, and he soon learns that there are two new pilots on a training flight, along with Doc Daneeka. No matter that Doc Daneeka is on the ground, watching McWatt's plane with the same curiosity as Yossarian and Sergeant Knight, and no matter that Doc Daneeka keeps insisting that "I'm right here." Since he's listed on the flight roster, he is officially in the plane. Meanwhile, McWatt's plane "kept climbing higher and higher." At one point

two parachutes pop open (the two new pilots) and thus the scene is set for
more grotesque dominos to fall:

> "Two more to go," said Sergeant Knight. "McWatt and Doc
> Daneeka."
> "I'm right here, Sergeant Knight," Doc Daneeka told him
> plaintively. "I'm not in the plane."
> "Why don't they jump?" Sergeant Knight asked, pleading
> aloud to himself. "Why don't they jump?"
> "It doesn't make sense," grieved Doc Daneeka, biting his lip.
> "It just doesn't make sense."
> But Yossarian understood suddenly why McWatt wouldn't
> jump, and went running uncontrollably down the whole length
> of the squadron after McWatt's plane, waving his arms and
> shouting up at him imploringly to come down, McWatt, come
> down; but no one seemed to hear, certainly not McWatt, and a
> great, choking moan tore from Yossarian's throat as McWatt
> turned again, dipped his wings once in salute, decided oh, well,
> what the hell, and flew into a mountain.

The suicidal gesture kills not only McWatt, but also Doc Daneeka who has
absolutely no luck convincing anybody that he is still alive. Since he *must*
have been killed in the crash, Doc Daneeka can no longer draw pay or PX
rations; he "found himself ostracized in the squadron by men who cursed his
memory"; and in due time his wife receives the following all-purpose letter
from Colonel Cathcart:

> *Dear Mrs., Mr., Miss, or Mr. and Mrs. Daneeka: Words cannot*
> *express the deep personal grief I experienced when your husband, son,*
> *father or brother was killed, wounded or reported missing in action.*

Mrs. Daneeka, flush with her husband's insurance monies and besieged by
suitors, is perhaps the last domino to fall on poor Doc Daneeka. When he
writes "begging her to bring his plight to the attention of the War
Department and urging her to communicate at once with his group
commander, Colonel Cathcart, for assurances that—no matter what else she
might have heard—it was indeed he, her husband, Doc Daneeka, who was
pleading with her, and not a corpse or some imposter," she is tempted to
comply. But Colonel Cathcart's letter (which certainly covers every possible
situation—and with "deep personal grief" to boot) clinches the matter: she
"moved with her children to Lansing, Michigan, and left no forwarding

address." That is how far the grotesque tentacles of a lazy afternoon on Pianosa when "something happened" can eventually reach; and such is the long reach of Death's arm in a novel where bureaucracy is a more efficient killing machine than German bullets.

Yet as horrible as these cascading dominos might be, they pale when compared to Yossarian's ill-fated rescue of Nately's whore's little sister. As a number of critics have pointed out, "The Eternal City" chapter is filled with resonances to Dante's vision of hell, but it is also a contemporary version of the Grail Knight out to rescue innocence from the clutches of a corrupted world. At this point in the novel Yossarian is AWOL, no longer a believer in Catch-22, no longer willing to fly missions (the number has skyrocketed to eighty), and given to "walking backward with his gun on his hip." Moreover, there are ominous signs of a general breakdown back at Pianosa: other flyers are beginning to grumble, and "there was a danger some of them might put on guns and begin walking around backward, too." Attitudes that had formerly belonged to Yossarian alone are becoming widespread. In short, he is no longer the odd man out, the one "crazy" enough to question the authority of Catch-22.

At the same time, however, Yossarian is beginning to move from an interest in mere survival to a position of moral responsibility. Victimhood alone no longer allows one off the hook: "Someone had to do something sometime. Every victim was a culprit, every culprit a victim, and somebody had to stand up sometime to try to break the lousy chain of inherited habit that was imperiling them all." And so, Yossarian's anxious thoughts turn to the young—to the little boys in Africa who "were still stolen away by adult slave traders and sold for money to men who disemboweled them and ate them"; to the poor young girls of Rome (a city with its Colosseum reduced to a dilapidated shell and its Arch of Constantine fallen) who have been chased into the mean streets; and especially to Nately's whore's little sister.

But the road from survivor to savior is not an easy one, especially when his increasingly desperate efforts to find the twelve-year-old virgin meet with knowing glances and offers to provide him all manner of young "virgins." Moreover, Rome's streets are swollen with suffering, drowning in cries for help: "The night was filled with horrors, and he thought he knew how Christ must have felt as he walked through the world, like a psychiatrist through a ward full of nuts, like a victim through a prison full of thieves." Even more significantly, the black humor that had both energized and sustained Heller's vision until this point gives way to passages as grim, as stark, as unrelievedly violent as any one can find in contemporary American literature:

At the next corner a man was beating a small boy brutally in the midst of an immobile crowd of adult spectators who made no effort to intervene. Yossarian recoiled with sickening recognition. He was certain he had witnessed that same horrible scene sometime before. *Déjà vu?* The sinister coincidence shook him and filled him with doubt and dread. It was the same scene he had witnessed a block before, although everything in it seemed quite different. What in the world was happening? . . . The boy was emaciated and needed a haircut. Bright-red blood was streaming from both ears. Yossarian crossed quickly to the other side of the immense avenue to escape the nauseating sight and found himself walking on human teeth lying on the drenched, glistening pavement near splotches of blood kept sticky by the pelting raindrops poking each one like sharp fingernails. Molars and broken incisors lay scattered everywhere.

In such a world human life is cheap, as Yossarian discovers when he learns that Aarfy has thrown an Italian girl to her death. Aarfy not only fails to register any remorse, but he argues instead that he really had no choice. After all, he had only raped her *once*, and, as he puts it, "I couldn't very well let her go around saying bad things about us, could I?"

Yossarian is astounded. Not only has he *not* found the girl he's been searching for, but he has arrived too late to protect, to "catch" the Michaela Aarfy tossed out his window like so much garbage. The moment cannot help but remind readers of another would-be protector of innocence, the Holden Caulfield of J. D. Salinger's *The Catcher in the Rye*, as well as Yossarian's meditation over Snowden's flak-riddled body: "Drop him out a window and he'll fall. . . . The spirit gone, man is garbage." The human damage done, all Yossarian can do is insist on justice: "You *killed* a girl," he tells the complacent, pipe-smoking Aarfy. "They're going to put you in jail."

But the brawny MPs who burst through the door aren't after Aarfy. Instead "they arrested Yossarian for being in Rome without a pass" and led him away with a grip "as hard as steel manacles." In a novel filled with contemporary versions of what William Blake once called "mind-forged manacles," there are also moments when physical grips restrain and literal bullets kill. But Heller manages to file even these under the broad general heading of Catch-22.

Like George Orwell's *Animal Farm*—which proves by an impeccable logic all its own that (a) all animals are equal and that (b) some animals are more equal than others, some of the absurdities in *Catch-22* are not only more equal but also more absurd than others. For example, given the bureaucratic noose that systematically tightens around Doc Daneeka's neck, Milo's machinations strike the same absurd tune, but one played in a very different key. After all, the apparent absurdity of buying eggs for seven cents apiece and selling them for five cents apiece is not, strictly speaking, an exercise in absurdity—at least as Heller's novel usually dramatizes the term; rather, it has the simplicity, and the cunning, of genius. In this sense Milo belongs in the same company as Major —— de Coverley, who deflates the cunning and terror of the Glorious Loyalty Oath Crusade with two simple words: "Gimme eat!" Thus, the absurdist reign of Joe McCarthyite machinations—with its reams of meaningless paper and manufactured suspicions—comes to an end.

Yet of all the characters who manipulate the system none is more insidious or more subtle than Orr. He is the one character in *Catch-22* with enough native horse sense and Yankee ingenuity, through old-fashioned pragmatism, to beat Catch-22 at its own game. He has endless patience, infinite resourcefulness, and best of all quiet confidence. One can hardly imagine two more unlikely roommates: Yossarian rails at an unjust world; Orr stuffs his cheeks with apples. Yossarian, of course, wants justice, while Orr, more modestly, will settle for "apple cheeks." Orr can spend happy hours assembling and disassembling the impossibly tiny parts of a valve so that they will have hot water in the morning.

However, beyond the world of their snug tent Orr is considered a loser, the sort of bad-luck pilot who crashes at the drop of a hat or the dipping of a wing. On one occasion—while Yossarian was still in the hospital after the first disastrous mission over Avignon—Orr's plane had apparently been hit and he "had eased his crippled airplane down gently into the glassy blue swells off Marseilles with such flawless skill that not one member of the six-man crew suffered the slightest bruise." Orr, in short, is a man who has raised the "crash landing" to a high art. Moreover, he apparently welcomes the chance to put the collected wisdom of survival manuals into practice—all the lore about chocolate bars and bouillon cubes, fish hooks, magnetic compasses, and little blue oars the size of a Dixie-cup spoon. Like Orr's tent standard-issue life rafts are jampacked with survival gear, and the infinitely patient, infinitely pragmatic Orr means to take full advantage of the possibilities. As Sergeant Knight describes the scene:

> I swear, you should have seen him sitting up there on the rim
> of the raft like the captain of a ship while the rest of us just
> watched him and waited for him to tell us what to do. . . .
>   Orr began opening up compartments in the raft, and the fun
> really began. First he found a box of chocolate bars and he passed

those around, so we sat there eating salty wet chocolate bars while the waves kept knocking us out of the raft into the water. Next he found some bouillon cubes and aluminum cups and made us some soup. Then he found some tea. . . . Whatever he found he used. He found some shark repellent and he sprinkled it right out into the water. The next thing he finds is a fishing line and dried bait. . . . In no time at all, Orr had that fishing line out into the water, trolling away as happy as a lark. "Lieutenant, what do you expect to catch?" I asked him. "Cod," he told me. And he meant it. And it's a good thing he didn't catch any, because he would have eaten that codfish raw if he had caught any, and would have made us eat it, too, because he had found this little book that said it was all right to eat codfish raw.

The scene warrants extensive quotation because it so clearly counterpoints Yossarian's epiphanic moment with the dying Snowden. For Yossarian the "truth" that Snowden represents is that man is mutable, that he must die, and this undeniable fact accounts for the death-haunted character of the novel's humor. If Yossarian's rebelliously playful tampering with Washington Irving/Irving Washington invokes the world of the tall tale, his obsession with death reminds us of the clear-sighted protagonist of Mark Twain's *Adventures of Huckleberry Finn.* Huck, of course, ends his tale by having to "light out for the territories" (a land Twain knew full well to be more lawless and brutal than the river towns along the Mississippi) rather than return to "sivilization." As he puts it, he had "been there."

By contrast, just at the moment when Milo and ex-PFC Wintergreen merge (in an image that betokens totalitarian control) and when even Yossarian finally realizes—after allowing Snowden's "secret" to burst full-blown from the unconscious, after his nightmarish and chronologically straightforward account of a journey to the hellish underworld of Rome—that "there is no hope for us, is there?" Heller provides an alternative, an *or.* As it turns out, Orr is alive and well after all. For the chaplain, "It's a miracle, I tell you! A miracle! I believe in God again." After all, what—other than divine intervention—could explain how Orr washed ashore in Sweden after being presumably lost at sea?

Yossarian, of course, knows better. Orr had *planned* his "evasion" to Sweden every bit as consciously, as persistently, as he had set about acquiring "apple cheeks." In a novel where people claim to see things twice, where vision itself is defined either as *jamais vu* (that condition of mind which accepts the strange as familiar) or as *déjà vu* (that condition which accepts the familiar as strange), Yossarian at last has the film on his own eyes stripped away:

> Don't you understand [Yossarian insists]—he planned it that way
> from the beginning. He even practiced getting shot down. He
> rehearsed for it on every mission he flew. And I wouldn't go with
> him! Oh, why wouldn't I listen? He invited me along, and I
> wouldn't go with him! . . . Now I understand what he was trying
> to tell me.

Armed with the fresh perspective called hope, Yossarian sets off for Sweden.
To be sure, he is only inches from the knife of Nately's whore, and at best
merely a shaky recruit to Orr's army, but at least he knows that Catch-22 is
not invincible, that it can be beaten. After all, who would accuse Orr of going
AWOL, of planning the whole thing? Nobody in their right mind
"rehearses" crash landings, and nobody imagines rowing—with an
implement as ludicrous as a "tiny blue oar"—to Sweden. It is all too absurd,
too outlandish—even for the world of Catch-22. But Orr does, and better
yet, he did.

Orr banks on the military establishment's general lack of imagination
rather like Milo relies on the inertia that always looks to Malta for its egg
supply. That is Orr's trump card. Moreover, he has raised the ante of
absurdity in ways that go way beyond mere accommodation. For Orr does
not merely want to make the best of a bad situation, nor is he especially
interested in gestures of protest. Rather, what he wants is the same thing that
ostensibly energizes Yossarian—namely, survival.

In a world brimming over with darkly comic deaths Heller's novel
moves beyond its broad canvas of biting social satire and grotesque,
cartoonish humor to embrace at least the possibility of individual triumph.
When others counsel caution or flat out tell him that he won't make it to
Sweden, Yossarian answers this way: "I know that. But at least I'll be trying."
In *Catch-22* the *trying* is all. Thus, Daniel Walden argues that Yossarian's
"desertion to Sweden was an act of faith, an act of opposition to irrationality,
a value-goal, an admirable attempt." It is all these, and perhaps more. For
Yossarian, like the Ishmael of *Moby-Dick*, is the man escaped to tell the tale—
of Kid Sampson and Doc Daneeka, of Colonel Cathcart and General
Dreedle, of Milo Minderbinder and ex-PFC Wintergreen, and of the all-
important Orr. And Heller has told his tale in ways that forever changed how
we think of "war novels" and the comic magic they can spin.

Chronology

1923   Born May 1 to Isaac and Lena Heller in the Coney Island section of Brooklyn, New York.

1941   Graduates from Abraham Lincoln High School in New York.

1944   Serves as a bombardier in the Army Air Corps.

1945   Marries Shirley Held. Publishes first short story in *Story*.

1948   Receives B.A. from New York University.

1949   Receives M.A. in English from Columbia University.

1949–50   Fullbright scholar at Oxford.

1950–52   Teaches composition at Pennsylvania State University.

1952–61   Works at various jobs, among them as a copywriter for *Time* (1952–56) and *Look* (1956–58) and then as a promotion manager for *McCall's* (1958–61).

1953   Begins writing *Catch-22*, his first novel.

1961   Starts teaching fiction and dramatic writing at Yale University and the University of Pennsylvania.

1961   *Catch-22* published.

1964   *Sex and the Single Girl*, written with David R. Schwartz, is produced.

1967   *We Bombed in New Haven* performed at the Yale School of Drama.

1968   *We Bombed in New Haven* performed in New York City and is published.

1970   *Dirty Dingus Magee*, a screenplay Heller co-authored, is produced.

1971   Distinguished Visiting Writer at the City College of the City University of New York. First performance of *Catch-22: A Dramatization* in East Hampton, New York.

1973   *Catch-22: A Dramatization* published.

1973   *Clevinger's Trial: A Play in One Act* (taken from *Catch-22*) published.

1974   *Something Happened*, a novel, published.

1979   *Good as Gold*, a novel, published.

1981   Becomes seriously ill from Guillain-Barré syndrome, a paralyzing nerve disorder from which he later fully recovered.

1984   *God Knows*, a novel, published. Divorced.

1986   *No Laughing Matter*, memoirs, written with Speed Vogel, is published.

1988   *Picture This*, a novel, is published.

1989   Marries Valerie Humphries.

1994   *Closing Time*, a sequel to *Catch-22*, is published.

1998   *Now and Then* published.

1999   Dies of a heart attack at his home in East Hampton, New York.

2000   *Portrait of an Artist, as an Old Man*, a novel, published.

Contributors

HAROLD BLOOM is Sterling Professor of the Humanities at Yale University and Henry W. and Albert A. Berg Professor of English at the New York University Graduate School. He is the author of over 20 books, including *Shelley's Mythmaking* (1959), *The Visionary Company* (1961), *Blake's Apocalypse* (1963), *Yeats* (1970), *A Map of Misreading* (1975), *Kabbalah and Criticism* (1975), *Agon: Toward a Theory of Revisionism* (1982), *The American Religion* (1992), *The Western Canon* (1994), and *Omens of Millennium: The Gnosis of Angels, Dreams, and Resurrection* (1996). *The Anxiety of Influence* (1973) sets forth Professor Bloom's provocative theory of the literary relationships between the great writers and their predecessors. His most recent books include *Shakespeare: The Invention of the Human*, a 1998 National Book Award finalist, and *How to Read and Why*, which was published in 2000. In 1999, Professor Bloom received the prestigious American Academy of Arts and Letters Gold Medal for Criticism.

FREDERICK R. KARL is a professor of English at New York University. He is the author of books on Kafka, Eliot, and Conrad and the contemporary English novel.

MINNA DOSKOW teaches at Rowan University in Glassboro, N.J. She is the author of *William Blake's Jerusalem*.

JAMES McDONALD has been a member of the faculty at the University of Detroit. He has published articles and poetry in various periodicals.

THOMAS ALLEN NELSON is a professor in the department of English and Comparative Literature at San Diego State University. He is the author and co-author of a number of books, among them *Shakepeare's Comic Theory: A Study of Art & Artifice in the Last Plays*.

STEPHEN L. SNIDERMAN is a professor at Youngstown State University.

CLINTON S. BURHANS JR. has taught at Michigan State University. He is the author of *The Would-Be Writer*.

DAVID H. RICHTER is a professor at Queens College of the City University of New York. He has written and edited numerous books on literature as well as rock musicians.

GARY W. DAVIS has taught at the University of Wisconsin and Emory University. He has written about critical theory and modern and contemporary literature, and is also the author of children's books.

LEON F. SELTZER taught at Cleveland State University until 1978, when he began a career in applied psychology. He has written a book on Melville and Conrad as well as essays on Dreiser, Faulkner, and Hemingway.

MARCUS K. BILLSON III has been in the English department at Oklahoma Baptist University. He is the author of a number of articles.

WALTER JAMES MILLER, Professor Emeritus at New York University, was for many years the host and producer of "Reader's Almanac" for the New York City municipal radio station. He has written critical studies of Heller and Vonnegut and annotated editions of *Catch-22* and *Twenty Thousand Leagues Under the Sea*.

SANFORD PINSKER is Shadek Professor of Humanities at Franklin and Marshall College. His books include studies on Conrad, Roth, and Ozick, and he has written collections of original verse as well.

Bibliography

Aldridge, John. "Contemporary Fiction and Mass Culture," *New Orleans Review* 1, no. 1 (Fall 1968): 4–9.

Aubrey, James R. "Major ——— de Coverley's Name in *Catch-22*." *Notes on Contemporary Literature* 18 (January 1988): 2–3.

Blues, Thomas. "The Moral Structure of *Catch-22*." *Studies in the Novel* 3 (Spring 1971): 64–79.

Brewer, Joseph E. "The Anti-Hero in Contemporary Literature." *Iowa English Bulletin* 12 (1967): 55–60.

Bronson, Daniel Ross. "Man on a String: *Catch-22*." *Notes on Contemporary Literature* 7 (1977): 8–9.

Canady, Nicholas. "Joseph Heller: Something Happened to the American Dream." *CEA Critic* 40 (1977): 34–38.

Cheuse, Alan. "Laughing on the Outside." *Studies on the Left* 3 (1963): 81–87.

Cockburn, Alex. "*Catch-22*." *New Left Review*, nos. 13–14 (January–April 1962): 87–92.

Day, Douglass. "*Catch-22*: A Manifesto for Anarchists." *Carolina Quarterly* 15 (Summer 1963): 86–92.

Denniston, Constance. "The American Romance-Parody: A Study of Heller's *Catch-22*." *Emporia State Research Studies* 14 (1965): 42–59.

Dickstein, Morris. "Black Humor and History." *Partisan Review* 43, no. 2 (1976) 185–211.

Fetrow, Fred M. "Joseph Heller's Use of Names in *Catch-22*." *Studies in Contemporary Satire* 1 (1975): 28–38.

Frank, Mike. "Eros and Thanatos in *Catch-22*." *Canadian Review of American Studies* 7 (Spring 1976): 77–87.

Frost, Lucy. "Violence in the Eternal City: *Catch-22* as a Critique of American Culture." *Meanjin Quarterly* 30 (December 1971): 447–53.

Galloway, David D. "Clown and Saint: The Hero in Current American Fiction." *Critique* 7 (1965): 46–65.

Gaukroger, Doug. "Time Structure in *Catch-22*." *Critique* 12, no. 2 (1970): 46–57.

167

Gordon, Caroline, and Jeanne Richardson. "Flies in Their Eyes? A Note on Joseph Heller's *Catch-22*." *Southern Review* 3 (Winter 1967): 96–105.

Greenberg, Alvin. "The Novel of Disintegration: Paradoxical Impossibility in Contemporary Fiction," *Wisconsin Studies in Contemporary Literature* 7, no. 1 (Winter/Spring 1966): 103–24.

Gross, Beverly. "'Insanity Is Contagious': The Mad World of *Catch-22*." *The Centennial Review* 26 (1982): 86–113.

Grossman, Edward. "Yossarian Lives." *Commentary* 58 (November 1974): 78, 80, 82–84.

Harris, Charles B. "*Catch-22*: A Radical Protest against Absurdity." *Contemporary American Novelists of the Absurd*. New Haven: College and University Press, 1971, pp. 33–50.

Hartshorne, Thomas L. "From *Catch-22* to *Slaughterhouse-V*: The Decline of the Political Mode." *South Atlantic Quarterly* 78 (1979): 17–33.

Hasley, Louis. "Dramatic Tension in *Catch-22*." *Midwest Quarterly* 15 (1974): 190–97.

Hassan Ihab. "Laughter in the Dark: The New Voice in American Fiction," *American Scholar* 33 (Autumn 1964): 636–39.

Heller, Terry. "Notes on Technique in Black Humor." *Thalia: Studies in Literary Humor* 2, no. 3 (1979): 15–21.

Henry, G. B. McK. "Significant Corn: *Catch-22*." *Melbourne Critical Review* 9 (1966): 133–44.

Janoff, Bruce. "Black Humor, Existentialism, and Absurdity: A Generic Confusion," *Arizona Quarterly* 30 (1974): 293–304.

Kazin, Alfred. *Bright Book of Life: American Novelists and Storytellers from Hemingway to Mailer*. New York: Delta, 1974.

Keegan, Brenda M. *Joseph Heller: A Reference Guide*. Boston: Hall, 1978.

Kennard, Jean. "Joseph Heller: At War with Absurdity." *Mosaic* 4 (1971): 75–87.

Kiley, Frederick, and Walter McDonald, eds. *A Catch-22 Casebook*. New York: Crowell, 1973.

Larson, Michael J. "Shakespearian Echoes in *Catch-22*." *American Notes and Queries* 17 (1979): 76–78.

Lehan, Richard, and Jerry Patch. "*Catch-22*: The Making of a Novel." *Minnesota Review* 7 (1967): 238–44.

Levine, Paul. "The Politics of Alienation." *Mosaic* 2, no. 1 (Fall 1968): 3–17.

Littlejohn, David. "The Anti-Realists." *Daedalus* 92, no. 2 (Spring 1963): 250–64.

McDonald, Walter R. "He Took Off: Yossarian and the Different Drummer." *CEA Critic* 36 (1973): 14–16.

McNamara, Eugene. "The Absurd Style in Contemporary American Literature." *Humanities Association Bulletin* 19, no. 1 (Winter 1968): 44–49.

Mellard, James M. "*Catch-22*: *Déjà vu* and the Labyrinth of Memory." *Bucknell Review* 16, no. 2 (1968): 29–44.

———. "Heller's *Catch-22*." In *The Exploded Form: The Modernist Novel in America*. Urbana: University of Illinois Press, 1980, pp. 108–24.

Merivale, Patricia. "*Catch-22* and *The Secret Agent*: Mechanical Man, the Hole in the Centre, and the Principle of Inbuilt Chaos." *English Studies in Canada* 7 (December 1981): 426–37.

Merrill, Robert. *Joseph Heller*. Boston: Twayne, 1987.

———. "The Structure and Meaning of *Catch-22*." *Studies in American Fiction* 14 (Fall 1986): 139–52.

Miller, Victor J. "Heller's 'Bologniad': A Theological Perspective on *Catch-22*." *Critique* 12 (1970): 50–69.

Miller, Wayne Charles. "Joseph Heller's *Catch-22*: Satire Sums up a Tradition." In *An Armed America: Its Face in Fiction*, New York: New York University Press, 1970.

Milne, Vicor J. "Heller's 'Bologniad': A Theological Perspective on *Catch-22*." *Critique* 12, no. 2 (1970): 50–69.

Monk, Donald. "An Experiment in Therapy: A Study of *Catch-22*." *The London Review* 2 (1967): 12–19.

Mullican, James S. "A Burkean Approach to *Catch-22*." *College Literature* 8 (Winter 1981): 42–52.

Muste, John M. "Better to Die Laughing: The War Novels of Joseph Heller and John Ashmead." *Critique* 5 (Fall 1962): 16–27.

Nagel, James. "*Catch-22* and Angry Humor: A Study of the Normative Values of Satire." *Studies in American Humor* 1 (1974): 99–106.

———, ed. *Critical Essays on* Catch-22. Encino, Calif.: Dickenson, 1974.

———, ed. *Critical Essays on Joseph Heller*. Boston: Hall, 1984.

Olderman, Raymond M. "The Grail Knight Departs." *Beyond the Waste Land: The American Novel of the Nineteen-Sixties*. New Haven: Yale University Press, 1972, pp. 94–116.

Pearson, Carol. "*Catch-22* and the Debasement of Language." *CEA Critic* 38 (1976): 30–35.

Podhoretz, Norman. "The Best Catch There Is." *Doings and Undoings*. New York: Farrar, Strauss, 1964, pp. 228–35.

Potts, Stephen W. *Catch-22*. Boston: Twayne Publishers, 1989.

———. *From Here to Absurdity: The Moral Battlefields of Joseph Heller*. San Bernardino, Calif.: Borgo Press, 1982.

Protherough, Robert. "The Sanity of *Catch-22*." *The Human World* 3 (May 1971): 59–70.

Robertson, Joan. "They're after Everyone: Heller's *Catch-22* and the Cold War." *CLIO* 19, no. 1 (Fall 1989): 41–50.

Ruderman, Judith. *Joseph Heller*. New York: Continuum, 1991.

Ryan, Marjorie. "Four Contemporary Satires and the Problem of Norms," *Satire Newsletter* 6, no. 2 (Spring 1969): 40–46.

Schopf, William. "Blindfolded and Backwards: Promethean and Bemushroomed Heroism in *One Flew Over the Cuckoo's Nest* and *Catch-22*," *Bulletin of the Rocky Mountain Language Association* 26 (1972): 89–97.

Scotto, Robert M., ed. Catch-22: *A Critical Edition*. New York: Delta, 1973.

———. *Three Contemporary Novelists: An Annotated Bibliography of Works by and about John Hawkes, Joseph Heller, and Thomas Pynchon*. New York: Garland, 1977.

Solomon, Eric. "From Christ in Flanders to *Catch-22*: An Approach to War Fiction." *Texas Studies in Literature and Language* 11 (Spring 1969): 851–66.

Solomon, Jan. "The Structure of Joseph Heller's *Catch-22*." *Critique* 9 (1967): 46–57.

Stanford, Les. "Novels into Film: *Catch-22* as Watershed." *Southern Humanities Review* 8 (1974): 19–25.

Stern, J. P. "War and the Comic Muse: *The Good Soldier Schweik* and *Catch-22*." *Comparative Literature* 20 (Summer 1968): 193–216.

Tanner, Tony. *City of Words: American Fiction 1950-1970*. London: Cape, 1971, pp. 72–84.

Thomas, W. K. "The Mythic Dimension of *Catch-22*." *Texas Studies in Literature and Language* 15, no. 1 (Spring 1973): 189–98.

———. "What Difference Does It Make?" *Dalhousie Review* 50, no. 4 (Winter 1970/71): 488–95.

Wain, John. "A New Novel about Old Troubles." *Critical Quarterly* 5 (1963): 168–73.

Waldmeir, Joseph J. *American Novels of the Second World War*. The Hague: Mouton, 1969. 160–65.

———. "Two Novelists of the Absurd: Heller and Kesey." *Wisconsin Studies in Contemporary Literature* 5, no. 3 (Autumn 1964): 192–204.

Walsh, Jeffrey. *American War Literature 1914 to Vietnam*. New York: St. Martin's Press, 1982.

Way, Brian. "Formal Experiment and Social Discontent: Joseph Heller's *Catch-22*." *Journal of American Studies* 2 (1968): 253–70.

Weixlmann, Joseph. "A Bibliography of Joseph Heller's *Catch-22*." *Bulletin of Bibliography* 31 (1974): 32–37.

Acknowledgments

"Joseph Heller's *Catch-22*: Only Fools Walk in Darkness," by Frederick R. Karl. From *Contemporary American Novelists*, edited by Harry T. Moore. © 1964 by Southern Illinois University Press. Reprinted by permission.

"The Night Journey in *Catch-22*," by Minna Doskow. From *Twentieth Century Literature* 12, no. 4 (January 1967): 186–93. © 1967 by IHC Press of Immaculate Heart College. Reprinted by permission.

"I See Everything Twice!: The Structure of Joseph Heller's *Catch-22*," by James L. McDonald. From *The University Review* 34, no. 3 (Spring 1968): 175–80. © 1968 by the Curators of the University of Missouri-Kansas City. Reprinted by permission.

"Theme and Structure in *Catch-22*," by Thomas Allen Nelson. From *Renascence* 23, no. 4 (Summer 1971): 173–82. © 1971 Catholic Renascence Society, Inc. Reprinted by permission.

"'It Was All Yossarian's Fault': Power and Responsibility in *Catch-22*," by Stephen L. Sniderman. From *Twentieth Century Literature* 19, no. 4 (October 1973): 251–58. © 1973 IHC Press of Immaculate Heart College. Reprinted by permission.

"Spindrift and the Sea: Structural Patterns and Unifying Elements in *Catch-22*," by Clinton S. Burhans Jr. From *Twentieth Century Literature* 19, no. 4 (October 1973): 239–50. © 1973 IHC Press of Immaculate Heart College. Reprinted by permission.

172 ACKNOWLEDGMENTS

"The Achievement of Shape in the Twentieth-Century Fable: Joseph Heller's *Catch-22*," by David H. Richter. From *Fable's End: Completeness and Closure in Rhetorical Fiction.* © 1974 by the University of Chicago Press. Reprinted by permission.

"*Catch-22* and the Language of Discontinuity," by Gary W. Davis. From *NOVEL: A Forum on Fiction*, 12, no. 1 (Fall 1978): 66–77. © 1978 NOVEL Corp. Reprinted by permission.

"Milo's 'Culpable Innocence': Absurdity as Moral Insanity in *Catch-22*," by Leon F. Seltzer. From *Papers on Language & Literature* 15, no. 3 (Summer 1979): 290–310. © 1979 by the Board of Trustees of Southern Illinois University. Reprinted by permission.

"The Un-Minderbinding of Yossarian: Genesis Inverted in *Catch-22*," by Marcus K. Billson III. From *The Arizona Quarterly* 36, no. 4 (Winter 1980): 315–328. © 1980 by the Arizona Board of Regents. Reprinted by permission.

"Joseph Heller's Fiction," by Walter James Miller. From *American Writing Today*, edited by Richard Kostelanetz. © 1991 by Walter James Miller. Reprinted by permission.

"Catch-22," by Sanford Pinsker. From *Understanding Joseph Heller.* © 1991 by the University of South Carolina. Reprinted by permission.

Index

DATE DUE			
		HPARW 810 .9 H36J	
JOSEPH HELLER'S CATCH-22			
8/01		$36.95	

HPARW   810
        .9
        H36J

HOUSTON PUBLIC LIBRARY
PARK PLACE